CONTEMPORARY IRISH TRADITIONAL NARRATIVES
THE ENGLISH LANGUAGE TRADITION

Ireland

Contemporary Irish Traditional Narratives

The English Language Tradition

Clodagh Brennan Harvey

UNIVERSITY OF CALIFORNIA PRESS
Berkeley • Los Angeles • Oxford

UNIVERSITY OF CALIFORNIA PUBLICATIONS:
FOLKLORE AND MYTHOLOGY STUDIES

Editorial Board: Eugene Anderson, Daniel Crowley,
Daniel Melia, Joseph Nagy, Maria Herrera-Sobek

Volume 35

UNIVERSITY OF CALIFORNIA PRESS
BERKELEY AND LOS ANGELES, CALIFORNIA

UNIVERSITY OF CALIFORNIA PRESS, LTD.
OXFORD, ENGLAND

©1992 BY CLODAGH BRENNAN HARVEY
PRINTED IN THE UNITED STATES OF AMERICA

Library of Congress Cataloging-in-Publication Data

Harvey, Clodagh Brennan.
    Contemporary Irish traditional narratives: the English language tradition / Clodagh Brennan Harvey.
        p.   cm. — (University of California publications. Folklore and mythology studies; v. 35)
    Includes bibliographical references and index.
    ISBN 0-520-09758-0 (alk. paper)
    1. Tales—Ireland—History and criticism. 2. Storytelling—Ireland. 3. Folk literature, Irish—History and criticism.
I. Title. II. Series: University of California publications. Folklore and mythology studies; 35.
GR153.5.H37   1992
398.2'09415—dc20   91-32402

The paper used in this publication meets the minimum requirements of American National Standard for Information Sciences—Permanence of Paper for Printed Library Materials, ANSI Z39.48-1984. ∞

Contents

Acknowledgments, vii

Introduction   1
   Evolution of the Present Study, 1
      Cultural Identity and Irish Folklore Studies, 1
      Personal Travels and Research Agenda, 3
      The Question of "Tradition," 5
   Background to the Storytelling Tradition, 7
      Ar Cuairt, 7
         Travelers and the Storytelling Tradition, 9
      Other Social and Occupational Contexts, 11
      Women and the Storytelling Tradition, 12
      Folklore and the Criterion of Orality, 13
      Preservation vs. Innovation, 14

One: Social Change and the Storytelling Tradition   20
   Modernization and Economic Change, 20
      Factors Effecting the Decline of Traditional Storytelling, 22
         Technological Innovations, 22
         Dance Halls and Public Houses, 25
         The Introduction of the Automobile, 27
         The Modernization of Homes, 25
         Education, Literacy, and the Decline of the Language, 28
         The "Death" of the Tradition, 31

Two: Folklore Collectors and the Irish Storytelling Tradition   37
   The Pivotal Role of the Collectors, 37
      Collecting in the Past, 37
      Folklore Collecting Today, 38

Self-Consciousness and the Storytelling Tradition, 42
  County Clare: A Symbiosis of Music and Storytelling, 42
The Influence of Eamon Kelly, 45
Limitations in the Documentation of the Tradition, 47

Three: The Current Status of the Two Language Traditions   53
Developments in the Study of Traditional Narrative, 53
Aesthetic Considerations in Traditional Storytelling, 54
  The Preeminence of the Irish Language Tradition, 54
  The English Language Tradition: Narrating and
    Narrators of *Scéalaíocht*, 58
  The English Language Tradition: Narrating and
    Narrators of *Seanchas*, 68
Final Considerations and Portents of Change, 74

Appendixes

I Questionnaire	85
II *Ar Cuairt* and Related Terms	89
III Glossary of Gaelic Terms	92
IV Selected Tales	94

    The Quarryman's Son, 94
    The Mac a hAon Fionn, 100
    Above and Beyond the End of the Earth, 107
    The Gentlemen's Agreement, 113

Bibliography, 119

Index, 125

Acknowledgments

The completion of *Contemporary Irish Traditional Narrative*, and the fieldwork upon which it is based, would not have been possible without the generosity, interest, and encouragement of many. First, I wish to express my deep gratitude to those in Ireland who gave so freely of their time, resources, and hospitality to help me in this research: the storytellers and others whom I interviewed; the staff of the Department of Irish Folklore at University College, Dublin, particularly Bo Almqvist, Séamas Ó Catháin, and Bairbre Ó Floinn; and the folklore collectors who are farther afield—Tom Munnelly, Liam Costello, James Delaney, and Seán Ó hEochaidh. I am also indebted to Pádraig Ó Héalaí, of University College, Galway, for kind words and useful information. In addition, I wish to express my thanks to the people I met or with whom I stayed all over Ireland whose kindness was virtually unlimited, whose company I enjoyed, and who made the period of my research profoundly memorable.

On this side of the Atlantic, I must thank the American Association of University Women for the funding I received as an American Fellow during the last year of my dissertation research. For help and encouragement at every stage, I thank Patrick Ford and Robert Georges. For assistance and encouragement during the last laps, I am grateful to Vincent Dunn, Linda Morley, and Eleanor Wachs. Special thanks are also due to Kris Holmes for her consistent generosity and her assistance in preparing the map. For their invaluable patience and technical support, I extend my thanks to Mary Hampton, Gloria Belmontez, and Michael St. Jean of UCLA Medical Center Computing Services. Finally, I wish to thank my family for their forbearance and support, particularly my mother, Elizabeth Harvey, and my sister, Eilish Hathaway, whose support in every way helped to bring this project to final fruition.

Grateful acknowledgment of permission to reprint copyright material is rendered to the British Academy for extracts from J. H. Delargy's "The Gaelic Story-Teller. With Some Notes on Gaelic Folk-Tales" (London, 1945). Thanks are also due to the California Folklore Society for permission to reprint parts of the Introduction and

Chapter Two which were published in an article entitled "Some Irish Women Storytellers and Reflections on the Role of Women in the Storytelling Tradition" in *Western Folklore* 48 (April 1989): 109-28. J. E. Caerwyn Williams has also granted permission to quote from Patrick Ford's unpublished English translation of the Introduction to Williams' *Y Storïwr Gwyddeleg a'i Chwedlau* (University of Wales Press, 1972).

INTRODUCTION

EVOLUTION OF THE PRESENT STUDY

The present work examines the condition of contemporary Irish traditional storytelling in the English language, including its relationship to traditional storytelling in the Irish language and to a panoply of factors that contribute to the tensions between urban and rural interests in Ireland today. The storytelling tradition in English and its exponents exist in a state of uneasy quiescence, caught between the tradition in the Irish language and current developments in English language narration at the level of popular culture. The state of the English language tradition is at once a reflection and a byproduct of the activities of the Irish folklore collectors and their role in the preservation of the tradition. It is this essential relationship that this study explores. Because Irish folklore collecting and scholarship have been essentially nationalistic in their thrust, I will begin this introduction with a brief overview of the genesis and techniques of systematic folklore collecting in Ireland and then progress to the evolution of the goals and the implementation of the research upon which this study is based. To place the results of this research within the traditions of Irish folklore scholarship, I first examine selected aspects of the social milieu of traditional storytelling as well as a number of long-standing assumptions about the tradition.[1]

Cultural Identity and Irish Folklore Studies

The founding of the Gaelic League by Douglas Hyde and Eoin MacNeill in 1893 and the awakening of an intense interest in Gaelic Ireland at the end of the nineteenth century were among the factors contributing to the rise of Irish nationalism and to the Easter Rising of 1916. Although technically unsuccessful, the devastating repercussions of the rising generated tremendous support for the cause of Irish independence and ultimately led to the Anglo-Irish War of 1919-1921, the Civil War of 1922-1923, and the establishment of a new nation and a new national government in 1927.

In the belief that the preservation of the traditional lore of the country was essential to the forging of a strong sense of cultural identity,[2] the Irish government founded the Folklore of Ireland Society (*An Cumann le Béaloideas Éireann*), a volunteer body, in 1926; this event represents the first organized effort to study the corpus of Irish oral traditions systematically. As the activities of the folklore collectors expanded, so, too, did governmental agencies charged with the same task: the Folklore of Ireland Society became the Irish Folklore Institute (*Institiúd Béaloideasa Éireann* [I.F.I.]) in 1930 and, finally, the Irish Folklore Commission (*Coimisiún Béaloideasa Éireann* [I.F.C.]) in 1935. The Commission was established for the express purpose of "collecting, cataloguing, and eventually publishing the best of what remained of Irish oral tradition," a tradition that was considered to be in decline.[3] The conscious suppression of Gaelic social institutions and traditions in the foregoing centuries—willfully imposed from without through the political domination of Great Britain—had engendered in many Irish scholars, writers, and people generally a deep sense of cultural loss, a loss epitomized in the decline of the Irish language. As E. Estyn Evans observes in *Irish Folk Ways*,

> during that time period [i.e., the last 150 years] the steady loss of the Gaelic language resulted in the loss of a great deal of information on local and regional life and of a vast store of oral literature in which the lore of an ancient civilization was enshrined.[4]

Largely because of this sense of loss, Irish folklore collectors have emphasized the collection of Irish language materials in the Gaelic-speaking areas of Ireland (the *Gaeltachtaí*), for these areas were considered to be the richest in certain forms of tradition and the material most in danger of perishing.[5] The intention behind their endeavors was to provide future generations with "a window on a wonderful, heroic, Celtic past"[6] and to preserve a legacy of the achievements of the old Gaelic order, the "real" Ireland.

This emphasis on the collection, documentation, and preservation of traditional materials, particularly those in the Irish language, has persisted in the work of the Irish Folklore Commission and has remained the major goal of Irish folklore studies in this century. Thirty years ago, noted Irish folklorist Caoimhín Ó Danachair stated that

> the main efforts of the Commission's workers have been directed toward the collection and preservation of the material, rather than its exposition; this has been made necessary by the ever urgent consideration that they are engaged in rescue work, taking the last opportunities of recording a *dying tradition* [my emphasis]. Secondary research work...must, for the time being, yield to the exigency of the more vital need.[7]

With the founding of the Irish Folklore Commission in 1935, the first full time folklore collectors went out into the field. (Their number has varied over the years, usually between seven and ten.[8]) The early collectors were trained in the use of the Ediphone machine and were responsible for the verbatim transcriptions of the material they recorded. These transcriptions then became the property of the Irish Folklore Commission, as did the diaries that the collectors were also instructed to keep. The full time collectors received their training from the Irish Folklore Commission at University College, Dublin, and were usually assigned to Irish-speaking areas in the vicinity of their homes where, ideally, they were already well known.[9]

(The Commission also employed several part time collectors who followed the same procedures; they were unsalaried but paid on the basis of material collected.)

The collecting work of the Irish Folklore Commission was guided in the past by the system of classification and investigation presented in Seán Ó Súilleabháin's *A Handbook of Irish Folklore*, published in Dublin in 1942.[10] This collectors' guide follows a question-and-answer format and covers fourteen major areas of folk culture; in its range it seeks to illuminate the totality of traditional life.[11] From its inception the work of the Commission was conceived to extend "to all forms of human thought and endeavor as these are remembered in popular tradition."[12]

The Irish Folklore Commission was incorporated into the University College, Dublin, as the Department of Irish Folklore in 1971. The department's goals and procedures have remained consistent since the days of the Irish Folklore Commission, although it now maintains a somewhat smaller staff. The work of the collectors continues to be guided by the interview format of Ó Súilleabháin's *Handbook*; emphasis is still placed on the documentation and preservation of material in the Irish language, although two of the present full time collectors (Thomas Munnelly and James Delaney) work almost entirely with English-speaking informants.

Personal Travels and Research Agenda

It was indeed the pervasive characterization of Irish oral storytelling as a "dying tradition" that initially attracted me as a researcher to the field of Irish narrative, but it was not the only stimulus for my interest in Irish traditional culture. All the members of my family, except my sister and I, were born in Ireland. My parents lived in England from 1934-1953 (where I was born), and then emigrated to the United States in 1953. In 1962 my sister and I were sent back to Ireland for our secondary education. It was during a visit to a friend's farm in Skibbereen, Co. Cork, in the summer of 1963 that I was first exposed to the kind of wit and verbal play that Irish country people enjoy; it made a lasting impression on me. My parents retired to Ireland in 1968, and I had made several subsequent, lengthy visits by the time I returned there for three months in the fall of 1981 to conduct independent research on various areas of Irish tradition, paramount among which was oral storytelling.

During this period I traveled extensively over most of the country; I also learned very quickly that one did not encounter "storytellers" as an everyday experience—at least not *scéalaí*, the narrators of the older and longer narrative forms (known collectively as *scéalaíocht*) to which I had been exposed through my graduate training: *Märchen* (*sean-sgéalta*), hero tales (*sgéalta gaisce*), Fenian tales (*finnscéalta*) and others. My conversations at this time with two such narrators in English and several other individuals who were interested either professionally or nonprofessionally in the Irish storytelling tradition led me to question the accuracy of the long-standing notion that the storytellers and the stories were "dying out," for it appeared that it was not uncommon for these and other storytellers to tell their tales specifically and solely to folklore collectors and other professionals interested in traditional storytelling. This development suggested that the emphasis has been on the wrong corpse, so to speak, for it was not the storytellers and their tales that were dying out, but rather the traditional contexts and audiences for such storytelling.

Moreover, the ultimate death of all the narrators of traditional stories would, in fact, bear little relationship to the "death" of the storytelling tradition of the past because, in the course of social change, the narrators have already outlived the normal, informal contexts associated with the performance of traditional narratives.

In October of 1983 I returned to Ireland for six months to determine the defensibility of this assessment of the situation. I focused initially on traditional storytelling in English because I am not a fluent speaker of Modern Irish. I was also primarily interested in the narrators (*scéalaí*) of the longer and structurally complex narrative forms (*scéalaíocht*) because these genres have been most highly prized by folklore scholars and collectors and have appeared most often in collections of Irish folktales. However, because of the difficulty I had experienced in finding such storytellers during my 1981 visit to Ireland, I decided to expand my research to include the tellers (*seanchaí*) of shorter, more realistic stories, which are recognizably traditional by their content, and of various types of personal experience narratives. These two classes of narrative, *scéalaíocht* and *seanchas*, constitute the two main divisions of traditional storytelling.[13] At a later stage in my research I realized that some comparison of storytelling in both languages might be beneficial to this study, so I began to interview narrators in the Irish language. These interviews indicated certain quintessential differences between the two traditions besides the obvious one of language, and revealed that the present condition of the storytelling tradition in English cannot be fully comprehended without comparison to the tradition in Irish. I also now feel that my early focus on storytellers who narrate in English proved an added advantage to my research, for it served to highlight the distinctions Irish folklorists and storytellers make between the two language traditions and the problems and implications arising from such distinctions.

During the six-month period of my research in 1983 and 1984, I interviewed and recorded forty-three individuals, including folklore collectors, storytellers in both languages (twenty-four), people to whom I had been referred as possible storytellers or significant tradition bearers, and individuals considered by others as knowledgeable about the storytelling tradition in their localities. The staff members of the Department of Irish Folklore at University College, Dublin, provided me with a considerable number of my references to storytellers. The rest I obtained in a variety of ways: from the storytellers themselves, from folklore collectors, and from people I met in chance encounters.

The questionnaire I devised when I began my research was designed to elicit information regarding three major facets of the tradition of oral storytelling as it exists in Ireland today: (1) the life histories of the storytellers; (2) the process of transmission of their stories; and (3) the repertoires of individual narrators. More specifically, I asked questions to elicit information in the following subcategories:

(a) the circumstances under which traditional stories were told in the past;
(b) the types of circumstances under which, and the individuals from whom, the narrators learned their tales;
(c) the audience or audiences to whom these tales were told in the past and are told at present;
(d) the changes the narrators perceive in the choice of tales that they tell or have told, and in the content of their narratives;

(e) possible changes in the contexts for storytelling over time, and the reasons—from the narrators' points of view—for such changes (familial, economic, social, religious, political, or others);

(f) the experiences of the storytellers with folklore collectors and the effects such experiences may have had on them and their narrating.

Finally, I also asked questions designed to elicit more subjective information, such as possible changes in self-concept or worldview experienced by such storytellers in response to changing social conditions (see Appendix I). The significant trends and anomalies that emerged from these areas of questioning are systematically examined herein.

Although my initial assumptions about the social isolation of contemporary traditional storytellers proved limited in minor respects, for storytellers in both languages narrate in other contexts and for individuals who are not folklore collectors, it is the central argument of this study that the activities of Irish folklore collectors cannot presently be regarded as ancillary or secondary to the storytelling tradition. The collectors must be recognized as the most important formal audience for traditional storytelling and as the most important factor in the continuation and perpetuation of the tradition. This is particularly true of traditional storytelling in English, as I will demonstrate (Chapter Two).

The Question of "Tradition"

Since the present analysis focuses on *traditional* storytelling, I reiterate what I mean by "traditionality" in this context. As noted above, the Irish storytelling tradition is divided into two major categories of traditional narrative, *seanchas* (*sean-*, "old") and *scéalaíocht* (*scéal-*, "story"). Generally speaking, *seanchas* refers to shorter, more realistic forms (including local and family history, tales about encounters with various supernatural beings, and genealogical lore), while *scéalaíocht* refers to long, structurally complex tales; there are also many subgenres in these two branches of the tradition. Although some narrators tell both kinds of tales, Irish storytellers have tended to specialize in one or the other.[14] In fact, more respect has usually been accorded the narrators of the longer tales (*scéalaí*).[15]

For a number of reasons it was occasionally more difficult than it might appear to determine who could rightly be considered a "storyteller." Several people I interviewed knew traditional stories and told them but were not considered by themselves or others to be "storytellers." Conversely, others who conceived themselves and were identified by their families and neighbors as storytellers had great difficulty—for a variety of reasons—in telling me any stories at all. All of the tellers of stories in English at least attempted to narrate coherently, but some of the narrators of stories in Irish simply would not attempt to tell me a story in English. (Although they were all fluent English speakers, a few did not *feel* fluent in the language.) Finally, in several cases, both the self-concept of storyteller and the reputation of being one developed specifically as a result of an individual's having been recorded by one of the collectors of the Irish Folklore Commission or the Department of Irish Folklore.

For the purposes of this research, therefore, I consider as storytellers individuals meeting one or more of the following criteria: (1) those individuals known as storytellers and considered such by members of their families, friends, neighbors, and others; (2) individuals whose stories have been recorded by collectors from the Irish Folklore Commission or the Department of Irish Folklore; (3) individuals who conceive themselves to be storytellers; and (4) individuals whose stories are of the kind the professional folklore collectors would call "traditional" on the basis of their content or structure (e.g., motifs, dramatis personae, or plot) but who, for whatever reasons, had not been previously recorded. All of the storytellers are either *seanchaí*, *scéalaí*, or both.

There is one final point I wish to make in connection with the participants in this study, and to which I will return at length later. During the time of my visit to Ireland in 1981 and for four months of my visit in 1983, I did not have an automobile at my disposal. While I relied on public transportation to a limited extent, by and large I hitchhiked everywhere. This meant that I talked to a considerable number of people on a day-to-day basis when I was in the field, and that there were many occasions on which I had to explain just exactly what I was doing in Ireland. In a great many cases the response involved some type of reference to Eamon Kelly, Ireland's foremost commercially successful storyteller, who was invariably referred to as "The Shanachie." There can be no doubt that Mr. Kelly has had considerable influence on contemporary, popular conceptions of the old tradition and the old storytelling style, at least for those who have had limited exposure, or none at all, to it.

Mr. Kelly's name is literally a household word; he has performed as a storyteller in every commercial medium since the 1950s. In his various radio programs, stage productions, books, and recordings, Eamon has reworked the image of the "traditional" storyteller and developed his own style in accordance with the demands of the medium of performance. He consciously utilizes and modifies traditional narratives for his performances and excels in short, humorous sketches of country life. The rather arch quality of his presentations is reminiscent of the tone present in the works of some of the earlier Anglo-Irish writers of the nineteenth and twentieth centuries, when folktales were a popular form of after dinner entertainment for the literate classes.[16] One result of Kelly's considerable public exposure is that for most people living in Ireland today, particularly the young and those who reside in urban areas, Eamon Kelly is the only person through whom they have been exposed both to Irish rural life and to the old storytelling tradition, an essentially rural phenomenon. It was certainly at least in part because of Kelly's influence that I had to be so careful about references to storytellers I received on a casual basis: Eamon Kelly imitators abound in Ireland. Moreover, I believe that it is due at least in part to Kelly's performance persona that the term *seanchaí* (English spellings seanachie, shanachie, and others), which has been used in English since at least the sixteenth century,[17] is rapidly becoming a blanket term for any type of "traditional" storyteller, "traditional" in this sense meaning associated with rural life. Mr. Kelly was kind enough to be interviewed as part of this research at the Abbey Theatre in Dublin on April 2, 1984, and his influence on Irish contemporary traditional storytelling will be discussed in greater detail in Chapter Two.

BACKGROUND TO THE STORYTELLING TRADITION
Ar Cuairt

Although it has been recognized by Irish folklore scholars that both city and town dwellers are bearers of traditional knowledge, folklore in general, and storytelling in particular, have always been associated with rural life.[18] Descriptions of the usual contexts that give rise to traditional storytelling in the countryside in Ireland are legion.[19] Even though there were several other significant contexts for storytelling, the custom of nightly visiting, known as *ar cuairt* (literally, "on a visit") and by many other names in both Irish and English (see Appendix II),[20] was the paramount form of social entertainment in most of Ireland until very recently. Household chat around the fireside provided the primary context for the telling of traditional tales and for learning the rules of decorum that governed such storytelling; the household itself was long the major forum for the acquisition and dissemination of traditional narrative material.

In Ireland the tradition of nightly visiting was confined mainly to the winter months when the hours of actual daylight were few and nights were long. Because weather conditions during the winter months were so severe, country people had some respite from the laborious demands of the agricultural cycle and more leisure time than they experienced during the other seasons. The introduction of television into rural Irish homes is a relatively recent innovation, the Irish television service (*Radio Telefís Éireann*) having been inaugurated in 1961.[21] Prior to that, people relied primarily on each other for entertainment during the long winter nights: they went visiting.[22] These evenings often included a variety of other activities besides storytelling, such as musicmaking, dancing, singing, cardplaying, and the discussing of local news and affairs. Certain houses in an area or village might be favored for such visiting, and available documentation of the tradition strongly suggests that it was primarily the men who were free to participate in these visits, the mobility of the women being limited by their domestic responsibilities, which did not end with nightfall.[23]

The following description appears in *Seán Ó Conaill's Book*, originally published in Irish as *Leabhar Sheáin Í Chonaill* in 1948 and translated into English in 1981. The narrator is Seán Ó Conaill, who lived in Cillrialaigh, on the Iveragh Peninsula, Co. Kerry:

> When the long nights would come long ago, the people of this and another village would gather together every night sitting beside the fire or wherever they could find room in the house. Many a device they would resort to shorten the night. The man who had a long tale, or the man who had the shorter tales (*eachtraithe*),[24] used to be telling them. At that time people used to go earning their pay in County Limerick, County Tipperary, and County Cork, and many a tale they had when they would return, everyone with his own story, so that you would not notice the night passing. Often the cock would crow before they would think of going home.[25]

This visiting was the primary context in which such narratives were heard and learned and in which the storyteller practiced and perfected his art.

The custom of nightly visiting did not disappear in any sense overnight, nor has it been discontinued completely. It has changed slowly, and in varying degrees, in different parts of the country. Although it is no longer the ubiquitous social phenomenon that it once was in the countryside, all the storytellers I interviewed in the course of this research, regardless of age, were participants in this aspect of the tradition or were exposed to it in a direct way. John Campbell, a noted storyteller living in Northern Ireland, was born in 1933, making him the youngest person to whom I spoke.[26] John describes at length the house in which he lived with his family when they first moved to Mullaghbawn, near Forkhill, in County Armagh. The house was well known in the locality as a *ceili* ("a visit") house:

JC: When we first come to Mullaghbawn here, we lived in a house over here—it was called "the salt box." It was a small little house, do you see?
CH: Was that a name you gave to it, or that local people called it?
JC: Everybody called it "the salt box."
CH: Because of its size?
JC: Because of its size. It had been just one bay first, and then somebody added on two more rooms, and it made it a sizeable house. But it still got the name "the salt box." And it was at sort of a crossroads—a "T-junction," you see. And it had always been a *ceili* house.
CH: Yes, right.
JC: There was an old man McCann lived in it, and the people always got the habit of going to it for *ceiliing*. The second night that we were in that house—at that time you lifted the latch. There was a half door, and you lifted the latch.
CH: Yes. I know the kind you mean, yeah.
JC: This big tall man, with a moustache, just lifted the latch and walked in.
CH: Who was that now?
JC: He says, "God save all in this house except the cat," do you see? And my mother looked 'round, and she says, "You're welcome." She didn't know who the man was at all. "You're welcome," she says. And he just pulled the chair up, and he sat in front of the fire.

The house maintained its reputation as a *ceili* house and, as a young boy, John heard there the several international folktales (among other kinds of stories) that he can still tell.

Many of the storytellers lived in areas in which one or several individuals were known for their storytelling ability. Jack Mahony lives in Cloonfad, Co. Roscommon, which is about three or four miles from Dunmore, Co. Galway, where John Reilly lives. John and Jack are distant cousins, and both learned stories from the narrating of John's father, also John Reilly. According to John, his father was an excellent narrator, and up to twenty people might arrive at his house on a winter night. It was from the senior John Reilly that Jack learned the international folktales and several of the other stories that he knows. Martin McKenna lives in Murrough, in Co. Clare, an area in which the decline of the Irish language has occurred fairly recently. Mr. McKenna can understand Irish perfectly, but no longer speaks it. He heard many stories from his grandfather, who lived with Martin's family, and who, according to Martin, was considered the best storyteller in the area.

Travelers and the Storytelling Tradition

Although there is little evidence of it today, in the past the roads of Ireland were traversed by wanderers of many kinds. James Delargy (Séamus Ó Duilearga), a pioneer in Irish folklore studies, noted a large number of these in his essay "The Gaelic Story-Teller," published in 1945: beggars, itinerant laborers (*spailpíní*), "poor scholars," cattledrovers, carters, poets and balladeers, pipers, harpers, fiddlers and dancing masters, soldiers, smugglers, and tradesmen of all kinds.[27] These multifarious vagabonds played an important role in the storytelling tradition, for they had many opportunities to hear and to tell tales, and they were often welcome visitors on the cold winter nights: "Stories were told by travellers such as pedlars, hawkers, beggars, poor scholars, and other itinerants of olden days who travelled habitually from one place to another throughout the country."[28]

Foremost among these nomads were the "tinkers" or "traveling people," who are also known by several other names that range from mildly to strongly pejorative. In *Puck of the Droms*, a recent collection of the narratives of travelers, itinerant Patrick Stokes gives this self-description: "Some of them calls us Travelers, Gypsies, or mumpers. Maybe, itinerants, tramps, or wasters. I heard them say no-goods, scoundrels, and *nackers*. But I'd say we're *minkers*, puck o' the droms."[29] The travelers practiced a multitude of trades typical of a nomadic existence, including horsetrading, tinsmithing, and various kinds of fortunetelling.

Although the narrative traditions of travelers per se have not received much scholarly attention until fairly recently, a considerable body of narrative has been recorded from Irish travelers. Many of them maintained fairly fixed routes and sought, or were aware of, houses in a locality where they might find welcome. Some carried their reputations as narrators with them, as Delargy notes:

> In return for a night's lodging, the 'travelling man' would entertain the family and the neighborhood with the latest news of fair and market, and with ballads and songs and stories he had learnt in his home district or acquired in his travels. If the 'traveller' was known as a storyteller, the house which he had selected for his night's lodging was soon packed to the door with people of the neighbourhood....[30]

The influence of the travelers on the storytelling tradition is not so remote as it might appear to us today, for several individuals involved in my research were cognizant of the traveler's role in the tradition or had some experience with them as storytellers.[31] James Delaney, a collector for the Department of Irish Folklore, made some interesting comments on this subject:

JD: Well, the storytelling. The background to the storytelling was that itinerants, what they call "travelers," they were storytellers...

CH: Yes, often.

JD: ...some of them. Because I remember an old man telling me, over here in Offaly, that a particular itinerant, or traveler, used to come periodically to the district. You see, there were different types of itinerants. There were itinerants who confined themselves, we'd say, to a twenty mile radius of some particular place. And they came back regularly.

CH: Yes, right.

JD: And when they came back they had houses where they were accepted, got hospitality. And they might stop in that area for a month or two, and they'd go around begging around the area. But this particular itinerant, anyway, was a storyteller. And when the word came to this district that he had arrived, all 'round went to that house, as long as he was in it. And he'd tell stories there at night time.
CH: How long ago was this you're talking about now?
JD: That would be...Thomas Horan was born in 1882.
CH: Uh-huh. So it's Thomas Horan you're talking about now.[32]
JD: Yes, and it was in his lifetime.
CH: Yeah. So...
JD: So it would have been around, I suppose, 1890, or 1900.

Patrick ("Pappy") McCarthy, a man to whom I spoke about the storytelling tradition in Gleninagh, Co. Clare, pointed out to me that it is only during his lifetime that newspapers have become readily available in the area. Before this, travelers were one of the important sources of outside news; they were welcomed for the news and the stories of all kinds that they had to relate. Brendan O'Donoughoe, a successful businessman living in Ballyvaughan, which is about four miles from Gleninagh, had the opportunity to listen to the storytelling of Paddy Sherlock, a West Clare traveler well known as a storyteller.[33] Brendan comments thus on his experiences:

CH: How long have you had the interest in the area around Ballyvaughan that you have now?
BO: Well, I suppose that I've had the interest for the last thirty years, thirty-five years.
CH: That's quite a while now. And you knew some of the storytellers in this area?
BO: Oh, yes, indeed. I knew them quite well. I used to go and visit them, in fact, and they used to tell me tales. But as a boy growing up that time, you know, I had little interest in...
CH: How many years ago would this be now, Brendan, that you're talking about?
BO: About thirty-five years ago, yeah.
CH: How old were you at that time, say...
BO: I was about twelve at the time, you know. I had a lot of time for these men because they had a lot of time for me.
CH: Yes. That's really what's missing now, isn't it?
BO: That's really what's missing now.
CH: People having time. But was storytelling still very vital in this area at that time?
BO: Oh, yes. It was indeed, yes.
CH: That isn't that long ago now, really. This is only...
BO: No, it's not. I had a very interesting experience some years ago in relation to a storyteller. His name was Paddy Sherlock.
CH: Was he from this area?
BO: No. In fact, he was a traveling man.

CH: An itinerant?
BO: An itinerant, yeah. And I used to—Paddy used to camp very near. I used to live over the road there, and Paddy was a regular visitor to the area, he and his family. And they used to camp off of the main road. And regularly every night—well, not every night, but possibly three or four nights a week—Paddy was there. If he was camping there for a week, I would visit him about, maybe, four or five times. And I would sit around the open turf fire, together with other people in the area. Mainly old people. We would sit around the fire, and we would listen to Paddy relate these stories.

Other Social and Occupational Contexts

Among my respondents several other social contexts were associated with storytelling, the most notable of these being the wake. In contrast to the somber occasions that wakes are today, Irish wakes of the past were the settings for all kinds of activities, including storytelling, singing, cardplaying, games, music and dancing, feats of strength and agility, pranks, and roughhousing of all kinds. Although many of these activities have died out completely, for the Catholic Church strongly disapproved of many Irish wake customs, the wake is still, for some individuals, a significant context for conversation and storytelling. There is general agreement that storytelling did not usually occur at wakes held for young people or children, as these would be occasions of great sorrow.[34] Other contexts cited in which conversation was likely to give rise to storytelling include weddings, occasions of illness, and "gatherings of any kind."

Although storytelling has most frequently been stressed as a leisure-time activity, a number of occupational contexts were also significant to the storytelling tradition.[35] I talked at length to Tomáisín Ryan (a narrator of stories in Irish) in Gleninagh, Co. Clare, about the area's fishing economy of the past. Tomás' father was a fisherman, and every morning some of the local fisherman would gather in his house, usually around 4:00 a.m., to ascertain the weather conditions before starting out. They might remain there until 6:00 or 7:00 a.m., talking and telling stories. With her marriage, Catherine Droney moved from Murrough, in west Clare, to Bell Harbour, in the north. Mrs. Droney liked to go down to the harbor and listen to the talk of the Irish-speaking men on the turf boats that came into Bell Harbour from the Connemara area of Co. Galway. It was from them that she heard some of the stories she knew. John Campbell, a storyteller in Forkhill, Co. Armagh, used to hear stories in the course of his workday when he worked in a flax mill. Seán Ó Duinnín, a storyteller in Irish living in Coolea, Co. Cork, has had several occupations, including that of shoemaker. Seán indicated that storytelling was likely to occur in the shops of tailors and shoemakers, for it was common for people to gather there in the evenings—the "workplace"—for storytelling, card playing, and other activities. Storytelling had been a common diversion among the caretakers of the Muckross Estate in Co. Kerry, where I talked to a number of retired workers. Éamonn Ó Donnghaile, of Carna, Co. Galway, is an excellent storyteller in Irish, as was his father, Bartley. Éamonn noted that it was customary for the farmers in the area to visit each others' fields during the day and for storytelling to arise in the context of such visits. Among groups involved in activities that contributed to the support of the household, such as thatching or making *súgáns* (straw ropes used for multiple purposes), storytelling was also likely to occur. In summary then, one could concur with J. E. Caerwyn Williams' observation that in Ireland "any circumstance that brought men together provided an opportunity for the storyteller."[36]

Women and the Storytelling Tradition

This brings us to a problematic area of Irish folklore scholarship. It seems reasonable to assume that in this quotation Williams is using the term *men* to refer exclusively to men, and not to women also, for the role of women in the storytelling tradition is anything but clear. In general, extant documentation supports two propositions: first, that women participated less in the storytelling tradition than men; and second, that women tended to be narrators of *seanchas* rather than the longer, multi-episodic forms. Also, the telling of heroic tales by women, especially tales of the Finn Cycle (*finnscéalta*), appears to have been negatively sanctioned. Concerning these points, Delargy states that

> the recital of Ossianic [Fenian] hero-tales was almost without exception restricted to men....There are exceptions to this rule, but still the evidence is unmistakable that the telling by women of Finn-tales was frowned upon by the men.
>
> *Seanchas*, genealogical lore, music, folk prayers, were, as a rule, associated with women; at any rate they excelled the men in these branches of the tradition. While women do not take part in the story-telling, not a word of the tale escapes them....[37]

Delargy goes on, in "The Gaelic Story-Teller," to present and discuss several women who excelled as narrators of both Fenian tales and *Märchen* (*sean-sgéalta*), but it is clear that he regards them as the exception rather than the rule.[38]

Most accounts of the participation of women in the tradition convey very little information concerning their activities except to say that it was unusual for the women to go visiting with the men. Williams, for instance, tells us that if a young woman were in the house when the men came to visit, she would usually go to another house: "...one could have an *áirneán bean* as well as an *áirneán fear*, one for women as well as one for men" (*bean*, "woman"; *fear*, "man").[39] However, it was not always possible for a woman to leave home if others came to visit, particularly a woman with children, for reasons that are apparent. The preoccupation of women with their domestic responsibilities has been posited as one of the factors limiting their opportunities to hear and to learn new tales, and thus to participate more actively in the tradition.[40]

Although it was not invariably the case, my own research confirms that men and women usually went visiting separately and that it was unusual to hear women telling heroic tales. While many of the narrators, men and women, reported that one or both parents would tell stories of various kinds, Donal Moore, in Kerry, was the only one to state that he had heard Fenian tales being narrated by a woman—in this case, his mother.

The essential problem concerning the participation of women in the tradition is the relative lack of documentation—prior to the twentieth century—of the tradition as a whole, and of the activities of women in particular. As Williams acknowledges,

> the fact that the number of women who drew attention to themselves as skilled narrators in the modern period is few cannot help being significant, although it is not easy to gauge the significance. What we must remember, of course, is that the storytelling tradition in Ireland...has been studied in the period of its decline, and it is not fair...to assume that its condition in the twentieth century reflects its state at the beginning of the nineteenth century any more than it reflects its state during the preceding centuries.[41]

The fact that the ratio of women to men among the storytellers I interviewed so disproportionately favors men (20:4 in total; 15:2 narrators in English) is likewise significant. The social constraints operating in the documentation of women narrators, in situ or otherwise, present, I believe, particular ethnographic problems. Although it may never be possible to rectify "the lacunae in the record," the examination of these constraints may in some way illuminate the problem of the vagueness of our conceptions of the role that women played in the tradition. I discuss these matters in Chapter Two.

Folklore and the Criterion of Orality

As I note above, storytelling has always been associated with rural life; so, too, has the notion of "orality" been intimately bound to our conceptions of the meaning of *folklore*.[42] In Ireland, however, assumptions regarding the origins of narratives in oral tradition can often be highly problematical. All the storytellers involved in this research (both English and Irish language narrators) learned stories from the oral narrations of others in the various contexts I have described herein. However, while a few of the narrators emphatically stated that they would not tell tales that they learned from books or other printed media because they were "not folklore," a surprising number know, have told, or tell tales that they originally read in or heard recited from printed sources. Seán Ó Duinnín, for example, an accomplished narrator in Irish, frequently performs tales he learns from printed collections, but only after he has "put his own Irish" on them. Seán regards the printed version of a tale merely as another version because so many of the tales that appear in collections were originally recorded from oral tradition.

It is noteworthy that many of stories that the storytellers knew from printed materials were those to which they were exposed as schoolchildren, most often in textbooks, but also in multitudinous commercial magazines and periodicals such as *Ireland's Own* (still in existence).[43] These publications included ordinary folktales, in Irish and English, as well as tales recounting the deeds of the important heroes of the Ulster and Fenian cycles, particularly CúChulainn and Fionn MacCumhail; such tales were both read and recited in the classroom. Because of the intense nationalism that pervaded Irish polity and literary endeavor at the beginning and well into this century, the thrust of much of the social and political agenda was to acquaint Irish people generally "with a nationalist version of the Irish past through propaganda and historical romances in the popular press."[44] This agenda was also manifest later in the policy of the Irish Department of Education, which instructed its teachers to inculcate their charges with the "Gaelic outlook" of Ireland's heroic past.[45] The themes, images, and characters of the early myths and sagas were among the vehicles used in textbooks and other printed sources to reinforce in children and young adults a sense of cultural identity and a respect for the achievements of the old Gaelic culture. Educational material of this nature is used even today in Irish children's textbooks to accomplish the same ends.[46]

Because of literally centuries of interplay between Irish oral and written traditions, and the complexity of the relationships between them, the problem of the oral versus the literary origins of Irish narratives has remained an issue in Irish folklore scholarship to the present day. The task of discovering whether a particular tale had its origin in oral tradition or in some printed source can often be a very difficult and painstaking one, as Séamas Ó Catháin points out:

> Only a dedicated folklorist, grappling with the problem of analysing and unravelling the complex relationships of a story which may have had several retellings since its first reading from the printed page, can hope to provide answers to such awkward questions as: how many tellings over how many generations suffice to convert such a story into a normal part of the corpus of oral tradition?[47]

The criterion of orality is of less concern to contemporary American folklore scholars, who, by and large, are more used to dealing with the effects of popular communications media on tradition and have recognized the role of popular media in the creation of folklore. The solution to the problem of "genuine" versus "spurious" folklore, if such is possible, is beyond the limits of this work; however, points to which I will return in Chapter Three are the facts that traditional stories have been learned and retold from both oral and written sources, and that both linguistic and media boundaries have been crossed in such retellings.

Preservation vs. Innovation

Another aspect of the storytelling tradition that I wish to discuss briefly is the conservatism that has always been associated with the concept of *traditional* storytelling. The overwhelming majority of the narrators I interviewed averred that they attempt to tell their stories in the same manner in which they first heard them; with the exception of personal experience narratives, they strive for fidelity to the original source of the tale.[48] In the storytellers' views, then, the tradition is a memorial one in which more value is placed on the preservation of the tradition than on innovation. In questioning them further concerning the circumstances under which they might make changes in a tale, several acknowledged that they would change some element if they judged it to be inappropriate for a particular audience (an audience of women or children, for example), or simply leave it out. By and large all attempted to tell stories they deemed acceptable to the audience at hand. Only a few individuals reported making deliberate changes in the stories that they tell, or making up stories themselves. Seán Ó Duinnín occasionally creates new stories, but shorter, humorous ones; Seán believes that to make up tales of the longer, multi-episodic kind would be to tamper with the tradition. Seán would also improve upon a story if he felt someone else's narrating to be somehow inadequate or inferior to his own. Seán is one of the few narrators who felt free to improve or embellish stories in their own retellings of them. Cáit O'Sullivan, a teller of stories in Irish, noted that she "never told a tale the same way twice"; she added that her mood or the circumstances affected her narrating and even, at times, her capacity to tell a story at all. Given these limited exceptions, the storytellers' own conceptions of their narrating involve a commitment to the reproduction of the original model of the narrative and, by extension, to continuity rather than innovation in the tradition.

A word must be said here on the problem of the current state of the Irish language. Generalizations concerning its moribund condition simply cannot convey the complexity of the situation as it is revealed at the local level and through the experiences of individuals. The implications of bilingualism as one finds it in Ireland are in fact multifaceted. Many of the storytellers learned their tales from English and/or Irish sources, sometimes oral and sometimes printed, and then elected to tell them in the language of their choice. Máirtín Lenihan, for example, is a narrator of stories in Irish living in Gleninagh, Co. Clare, an area which has only recently become almost all English speaking. Máirtín learned his stories from a man who first read them in books in English and then went on to tell them locally in Irish. In 1984 Máirtín told several of these stories to me in English for the first time.

The present work is an investigation of the contemporary Irish storytelling tradition as it exists for, and is experienced by, narrators of stories in the English language. The results of the research upon which it is based are organized and presented in the following fashion: in Chapter One, "Social Change and the Storytelling Tradition," I present the narrators' views on the changes they perceive to have occurred in the storytelling tradition during their lifetimes and the reasons accounting for such changes. A map of Ireland (frontispiece) provides the reader with a geographical frame of reference in which to situate the people and the localities that figure prominently in the discussions. In Chapter Two, "Folklore Collectors and the Irish Storytelling Tradition," I first analyze the crucial role of professional folklore collectors in maintaining and perpetuating Irish traditional storytelling, particularly storytelling in English. Second, I delineate two processes revealed in the course of this research by which several passive bearers of tradition came to the fore as active storytellers; I then discuss the changes in the tradition and in the general populace which I believe account for their acceptance in this role. Third, I also examine the problems and implications of the current absence of an informed audience for traditional narrating in English. In the final chapter, "The Current Status of the Two Language Traditions," I examine the present status of narrators in the English language tradition relative to that of their counterparts in the Irish language; I also argue that one of the causes of the preferential treatment accorded the narrators of traditional stories in Irish may be the difficulty of establishing aesthetic criteria for assessing traditional storytelling in English. In conclusion I suggest some of the external forces I believe are indicators of potential change in the storytelling tradition in English and its related scholarship. These include (1) the recognition by Irish folklore scholars that urban belief tales represent an important new form of folklore and, by implication, that new folklore genres can develop, and (2) the possible influence on the Irish storytelling tradition of the urban storytelling revival in the United States and elsewhere.

An important aspect of the analysis of the differences between the two language traditions in the final chapter is the discussion of the difficulty of establishing the aesthetic criteria for traditional storytelling in English. In order to make some general points about storytelling of this kind, the chapter also includes commentary on the narrating style and characteristics of particular storytellers (Packie Murrihy, Donal Moore, John Campbell, Francie Kennelly, Junior Crehan, and John Reilly) as well as selected narratives or segments of narratives from their repertoires. (Appendix IV contains the complete transcriptions of tales only partially presented in the text.) The words of the storytellers are presented verbatim, including false starts, hesitations, and repetitions, but for the sake of coherence and brevity I exclude almost all of my interjections and commentary and that of any others who may have been present at the recording sessions unless it seems essential to the understanding of what follows. Because extraneous vocalizations are infinitely more distracting in print than in normal conversation, verbatim transcriptions often do considerable injustice to the storytellers. However, I feel this mode of presentation best serves my purpose here, which is to reveal the difficulty of making aesthetic judgments of contemporary Irish traditional storytelling in English.[49]

Notes to the Introduction

1. The focus of this study is the present state of traditional storytelling rather than the evolution of Irish folklore studies or the literary uses of traditional narrative material. Both subjects have received extensive treatment elsewhere. Richard M. Dorson's "Foreword" to *Folktales of Ireland*, ed. Sean O'Sullivan (Chicago: University of Chicago Press, 1966), pp. v-xxxii, provides an in-depth survey of historical developments within Irish folklore studies as well as an analysis of the ways in which traditional narratives have been treated by writers of popular fiction. The "Introduction" to Henry Glassie's recent collection, *Irish Folktales* (New York: Pantheon Books, 1985), pp. 5-29, presents a very useful overview of the ways in which folktales have been treated by Anglo-Irish writers of popular fiction (T. Crofton Croker, William Carleton, John Millington Synge, et al.) as well as more rigorous scholars. Glassie's "Introduction" complements Richard Dorson's "Foreword" so that together they provide a comprehensive discussion of developments in Irish folklore scholarship.
2. Glassie, *Irish Folktales*, p. 20.
3. O'Sullivan, "Introduction" to *Folktales of Ireland*, p. xxxiii.
4. E. Estyn Evans, *Irish Folk Ways* (London: Routledge and Kegan Paul, 1957), p. 2.
5. A small information sheet entitled "The Department of Irish Folklore," published by the Department at University College, Dublin, states that "about three quarters of the main collection of lore is in the Irish language" (no date).
6. Caoimhín Ó Danachair, "Oral Tradition and the Printed Word," *Irish University Review* 9 (Spring 1979): 32.
7. Caoimhín Ó Danachair, "The Irish Folklore Commission," *The Folklore and Folk Music Archivist* 1 (Spring 1961): 4.
8. O'Sullivan, "Introduction," p. xxxiv.
9. Bo Almqvist, "The Irish Folklore Commission: Achievement and Legacy," *Béaloideas* 45-47 (1977-79): 7.
10. Seán Ó Súilleabháin, *A Handbook of Irish Folklore* (Dublin: Folklore of Ireland Society, 1942; reprint ed., Hatboro, Penn.: Folklore Associates, 1963).
11. The fourteen major categories of the *Handbook* are as follows: Settlement and Dwelling, Livelihood and Household Support, Communication and Trade, The Community, Human Life, Nature, Folk Medicine, Time, Principles and Rules of Popular Belief and Practice, Mythological Tradition, Historical Tradition, Religious Traditions, Popular Oral Literature, and Sports and Pastimes.
12. Ó Danachair, "The Irish Folklore Commission," p. 1.
13. These two divisions of Irish narrative are discussed in detail in J. E. Caerwyn Williams' book on the Irish storytelling tradition, *Y Storïwr Gwyddeleg a'i Chwedlau* (Cardiff: University of Wales Press, 1972). Professor Patrick K. Ford of UCLA made his unpublished English translation of Williams' introduction available to me. For future reference I will refer to Ford's translation as *The Irish Storyteller and His Tales*, which is Ford's translation of the Welsh title, and/or as "Williams [Ford]." Williams states that "it is fair to take *scéalaíocht* as the name of everything left after pulling *seanchas* out of the oral tradition." Williams [Ford], p. 84.

14. Williams [Ford], pp. 84-85.

15. Ibid., p. 105.

16. As Henry Glassie notes, at this time "the humorously sketched folktale was...a popular upper-class oral genre, appropriate for after dinner entertainment." Glassie, *Irish Folktales*, p. 14.

17. The Oxford English Dictionary cites examples of the use of seanachie (in many of its variant spellings) as far back as 1534, when it appeared in the state papers of Henry VIII. See *The Oxford English Dictionary*, 1961 ed., s.v. "Sennachie."

18. That folklore and folk narrative are essentially rural phenomena is not an assumption of Irish folklore scholars only; it has been a basic underpinning of folklore research in general since the work of the Brothers Grimm. A formulation of this construct is to be found in the "Instructions to Collectors" in Ó Súilleabháin's *A Handbook of Irish Folklore*, p. xi, which states, "Even city and town-born individuals possess traditional information concerning the ways and doings of those about them. It is in the country districts, however, that information is to be attained in greatest abundance."

19. Descriptions of rural Irish visiting patterns and contexts for storytelling are to be found, for example, in J. H. Delargy, "The Gaelic Story-Teller. With Some Notes on Gaelic Folk-Tales," *Proceedings of the British Academy* 31 (1945): 192-203; and *Seán Ó Conaill's Book*, ed. Séamus Ó Duilearga, trans. Máire MacNeill (Baile Átha Cliath: Comhairle Bhéaloideas Éireann, 1981), pp. xvii-xxi.

20. Because I believe the information may be of use to folklore and literary scholars, I have listed in Appendix II all the terms and expressions I encountered in both English and Irish which refer in some way to the custom of nightly visiting. The reader will notice that the English suffixes for actions ("-ing") and agents ("-ers") are frequently used with Irish words.

21. By 1965 more than half the homes in Ireland had television sets. Kenneth Neill, *The Irish People: An Illustrated History* (New York: Mayflower Books, 1979), p. 212.

22. Although radio broadcasts in Ireland began much earlier than television transmissions, television sets were purchased by a far greater percentage of the population in a much shorter period of time than was true of radios. According to Terence Brown in *Ireland: A Social and Cultural History, 1922-79* (Glasgow: Fontana, 1981), p. 153, the majority of radio licenses issued in Ireland at the end of the 1930s went to people living in Dublin and its environs; very few were issued for sets in Ulster and Connacht.

23. Seán Ó hEochaidh (Sean O'Haughey), the former folklore collector, suggested to me that the preoccupation with domestic responsibilities limited the amount of time women could spend listening to folktales and, by extension, learning and telling them (personal conversation, December 31, 1983).

24. This is the plural form of *eachtra* ("adventure"), often used synonymously with *seanchas*.

25. Séamas Ó Duilearga, ed., *Seán Ó Conaill's Book*, p. xviii.

26. This is John's real name. However, I have used pseudonyms for many of the storytellers discussed in this study either to protect their privacy because of their advanced age or because, in my judgment, they seem to wish to avoid—or even shun—further notoriety.

27. Delargy, "The Gaelic Story-Teller," pp. 198-203.

28. Michael Corduff, "Notes on Storytellers and Storytelling in Iorrus, North Mayo," *Béaloideas* 19 (November-December, 1949): 177.

29. Artelia Court, *Puck of the Droms* (Berkeley and Los Angeles: University of California Press, 1985), p. 87.

30. Delargy, "The Gaelic Story-Teller," p. 199.

31. See also Lawrence Millman, *Our Like Will Not Be There Again* (Boston: Little, Brown & Co., 1977), pp. 85-102. Millman spent some time in Ireland tracking down and talking to old storytellers. He includes a discussion of some itinerants and their stories in this book about his experiences in Ireland.

32. Mr. Horan is James Delaney's informant, who provided the information about these practices, and not one of the itinerants being referred to.

33. For a collection of Paddy Sherlock's stories, see Séamus Ó Duilearga, "Paddy Sherlock's Stories," *Béaloideas* 30 (1962): 1-75. Included is biographical information about Mr. Sherlock.

34. This seems commonsensical. See Delargy, "The Gaelic Story-Teller," p. 194. For a full treatment of activities at Irish wakes in the past, see Seán Ó Súilleabháin, *Irish Wake Amusements* (Dublin and Cork: The Mercier Press, 1967), which contains a section on storytelling, pp. 26-27.

35. According to Williams in *The Irish Storyteller and His Tales*, "It is fair to assume that storytelling in Ireland was a means of entertainment during leisure time for the most part, not a diversion during work." Williams [Ford], p. 71.

36. Williams [Ford], p. 64.

37. Delargy, "The Gaelic Story-Teller," p. 181.

38. Ibid., pp. 181-182, 189.

39. Williams [Ford], p. 59.

40. Máire Nic Aodha (a narrator of stories in Irish living in Co. Donegal) described to me in considerable detail the domestic activities of her grandmother (with whom she lived as a child) which kept her grandmother at home in the evenings.

41. Williams [Ford], p. 75.

42. Thirteen of the twenty-one definitions in *Funk and Wagnalls Standard Dictionary of Folklore, Mythology, and Legend* include the notion of "orality" as a defining criterion for folklore. *Funk and Wagnalls Standard Dictionary of Folklore, Mythology, and Legend*, 1972 ed., vol. 1, s.v. "Folklore."

43. *Ireland's Own: A Journal of Fiction, Literature, and General Information* (Dublin: n.p., 1902—present).

44. Martin J. Waters, "Peasants and Immigrants: Considerations of the Gaelic League as a Social Movement," in *Views of the Irish Peasantry*, ed. Daniel J. Casey and Robert E. Rhodes (Hamden, Conn.: Archon Books, 1977), p. 165.

45. Michele Capolungo, "The Heritage of the Cuchulain Legend in the Modern Irish Ireland of W. B. Yeats and P. H. Pearse" (Master's thesis, Centre de Recherches Théâtre et Société, Université de Provence - Centre d'Aix), p. 90.

46. For an example of a textbook of this kind, see Seán Ó Domhnaill, *Seal ag Léamh* [Reading Time] (Baile Átha Cliath: An Comhlacht Oideachais, 1977), pp. 52-54, which contains a child's version of the story of how CúChulainn received his name with exercises on the story (all in Irish); it is currently used in the primary school curriculum. In his doctoral dissertation, Arthur Gribben discusses in detail the ways in which educational and commercial publications inform the sense of local identity and popular consciousness in children and adults who live in the area of Ireland (north Co. Louth) in which some of the central events of the *Táin Bó Cuailnge*, Ireland's foremost heroic epic, purportedly occurred. See Arthur Gribben, "The Role of the Ancient Epic *Táin Bó Cuailnge* in the Sense of Local Cultural Identity in Contemporary North County Louth, Ireland" (Ph.D. diss., University of California, Los Angeles, 1988).

47. Séamas Ó Catháin, *The Bedside Book of Irish Folklore* (Dublin and Cork: The Mercier Press, 1980), p. 12.

48. That this notion of "perfect fidelity" is at best a highly problematic construct is discussed throughout Seán Ó Coileáin's article, "Oral vs. Literary? Some Strands of the Argument," *Studia Hibernica* 17-18 (1977-78): 7-35 (particularly pp. 11-22).

49. The complete transcriptions of the stories, including the comments of all present, can be found in my doctoral dissertation. See Clodagh Margaret Harvey, "A Contemporary Perspective on Irish Traditional Storytelling in the English Language" (Ph.D. diss., University of California, Los Angeles, 1987). It also contains fifteen sections on individual narrators of stories in English (including Donal Moore, who narrates in Irish as well). These sections all include the following: (1) information about the ways in which the narrators came to my attention and how I contacted them; (2) basic biographical data (such as education, occupational experience, domicile, marriage and children); (3) a discussion of the narrators' participation in the storytelling tradition and experiences with folklore collectors; and (4) transcriptions of representative examples from the repertoires of the storytellers, with extensive documentation and commentary on the selected stories.

1

SOCIAL CHANGE AND THE STORYTELLING TRADITION

MODERNIZATION AND ECONOMIC CHANGE

As noted in the Introduction, an important part of the field research on which this study is based was the systematic interviewing of narrators as well as individuals informed about the Irish storytelling tradition ("nonnarrators"). I used the same basic questionnaire for interviews with narrators and nonnarrators, but my discussions with nonnarrators, particularly folklore collectors, were generally less directed than those with storytellers and tended to cover a wider range of topics, including those of more interest to scholars or items not covered in the questionnaire. The following discussion is based on research conducted in those areas of Ireland where I was able to locate both storytellers and individuals knowledgeable about the tradition.[1]

Some surprising results emerged from these interviews, particularly in two areas. First, although I do not really know why, I had expected considerably more variety in the life experiences of the narrators than was the case. In their broad outlines their lives are quite similar and correspond to a distinct and rather simple pattern; at least they share many characteristics. Second, all the narrators were questioned about the changes they experienced, over time, in the social situations in which they told their stories and about the reasons they perceived to account for such changes. I had assumed that "modernization," at least in the sense of "dependence upon technology" or a desire to "keep up with the times," would figure prominently as one of the causes for such changes. But I had also expected that, for some at least, familial, religious, economic, political, or other aspects of life would be important factors as well. This was not the case. To my surprise, the overwhelming response of most of the interviewees to questions about this kind of social change was "modernization," or some aspect of it.

The term "modernization" is, of course, a sweeping one that does little on its own to explain effects that seem to be taken for granted. However, it is not "all things to all men"; a closer examination of many of the views and explanations proffered during these interviews, by both narrators and nonnarrators, will reveal the particular meaning that "modernization" has for individuals. Because the modernization of the countryside is inherently linked to a rising standard of living, I will begin with a brief overview of the economic changes Ireland has undergone in the course of this century.

The present standard of living in Ireland represents a radical departure from that of the not-too-distant past. During preceding centuries, Irish life was essentially rural and agricultural and, except for a small minority of city and town dwellers, the whole nation belonged to one class, the so-called "peasant" class.[2] For many, daily life was maintained at a bare, subsistence level, and poverty was a pervasive characteristic of life in the Irish countryside. Numerous commentators have noted the poverty of Irish people in the past relative to those in the other countries of Europe. Paul Johnson comments thus in his recent history of Ireland: "By the 1830s it was generally believed that the Irish peasantry was the poorest in Western Europe."[3] This situation had not changed much for the better even well into the current century. Historian Michael J. Shiel assesses the plight of the small farmers in Ireland in the 1930s and 1940s:

> Clearly, many small farmers were living in near poverty. Following the failure of the potato crop and the Great Famine of a century earlier, Irish farming had moved away from the intensive tillage systems and towards a heavy dependence on livestock rearing. The switch to low-intensity cattle production...was not the kind of enterprise to generate high farm incomes and indeed it was badly suited to the small farm, particularly on the poor soils of the west.[4]

Ireland began to experience an economic revival in the 1960s and this, accelerated by Ireland's entrance into the European Economic Community (the "Common Market") in 1973, resulted in tremendous economic advancement and growth, and a dramatic rise in the standard of living, in a relatively short period of time. In 1977 alone, Ireland's Gross National Product (GNP) increased seven percent, giving it one of the largest rates of growth in the world.[5]

The traditional storytellers I encountered, both Irish speakers and English speakers, have as a consequence experienced a great deal of change during their lifetimes and have been directly affected by this economic rejuvenation. All of them now, as a result of their own endeavors or of protective measures implemented by the Irish government, or a combination of both, live in at least relative economic security. The government guarantees, and often provides, older people with suitable places to live. They are given free use of public transportation, and health care is regularly available at negligible cost. In general, they are well taken care of in old age.

In spite of this rapidity of social change, all of the storytellers represent some continuity with the storytelling tradition of the past, both experientially and symbolically. On the level of personal experience, all have, regardless of age, participated in *ar cuairt* ("on a visit") or in the other contexts for traditional storytelling described herein.[6] At a more symbolic level, the pattern that emerged from the interviews reveals much continuity with the conventional and, by now, somewhat idealized notions scholars have presented of the lives of rural storytellers of the past: that of a constrained and toilsome existence mitigated by the joy of human companionship, of which storytelling was a part. The poverty in which the majority of Irish people have existed in the past, and even in this century, was experienced by many of the narrators. They have often come from and/or have been the parents of large families. They have had to struggle to support themselves and their dependents—often at multiple jobs—at a very minimal economic level. Finally, often having had only basic formal education, they have tended to live and work within a given area or locale for most of their lives and, frequently, to have worked for others (including their parents) rather than just for themselves (i.e., having their own farms or businesses). Many have, in a very real sense, seen Ireland virtually dragged into the twentieth century. As Henry Glassie aptly observes in *Passing the Time in Ballymenone*, his recent study of a contemporary community and its traditions in Northern Ireland, "these old storytellers watched the birth of the world you and I accept as given."[7]

Factors Effecting the Decline of Traditional Storytelling

Technological Innovations

"Modernization," then, was the overwhelming response to questions dealing with the possible reasons or causes for alterations in the contexts for traditional storytelling. Everyone I interviewed during this research, narrators and nonnarrators, experienced and perceived changes in the custom of nightly visiting, and its relationship to the storytelling tradition, in the localities in which they lived. Most frequently, the introduction of radio (the "wireless") and the television (which occurred considerably later) were cited as the major factors in the breakdown of the visiting patterns. These two media provided country people with inducements to remain at home on those cold, dark winter nights and, consequently, they were no longer so dependent on their neighbors for entertainment and diversion.

The responses to my investigation of this subject, which were more complex and diverse than I anticipated, have been codified in table 1.

Table 1. Causes of Changes in the Tradition

Television	11	Radio and Television	8
Radio	1	Television more influential	4
Radio more influential	1	Emigration	3
Automobile	2	Modernization of homes	2
Pubs	3	Various entertainments	2
Dances	2	Phonograph	1
Education	2	Newspapers	2
Bicycle/Radio/Television	2	"Women"	1
Decline of the language (Irish)	1		

As the information in the table reveals, two media of communication—radio and television—were collectively cited as the most important reason for the changes in the visiting patterns in the countryside. However, there was considerable divergence of opinion as to the relative weight that should be given to the importance of either. As the table shows, television was cited in general as (1) the main *single* factor accounting for these changes, and (2) by some, as *more* influential than, but coupled with, the importance of the radio. In terms of the radio, one respondent in Menlo, Co. Galway, felt that it was the single most important reason for social change. On the other hand, two others in Galway and Clare felt that the radio had little effect on the visiting patterns because people do not "watch" it in the same way they do television. (The latter responses do not appear in the table because they are not susceptible of measurement in terms of the categories.)

These variations in personal opinion are not of primary importance here, and they can be accounted for, in part, by the demographics of the larger social picture. To begin with, although Irish radio broadcasts began considerably earlier than television transmissions (from Dublin in 1926 and from Cork in 1927), the radio did not penetrate rural communities with the same rapidity or in the same density as did television. By the end of the 1930s, Dublin and the surrounding areas contained the highest single concentration of the radio sets licensed in Ireland (forty percent), with very few in either Ulster or Connacht.[8] When the national standard of living began to rise in the 1960s, the gap between rural and urban living standards also began to close; within only a decade of the inauguration of the Irish television service (*Radio Telefís Éireann*) in 1961, there was a television set in almost every house in the Irish countryside.[9] As I noted previously, a much larger segment of the population came to possess television sets within a much shorter period of time than was true of the radio. The importance of the opinions reported here lies less in their historical accuracy than in the fact that they reveal the tremendously rapid impact that television had on Irish people and Irish life.

The opinions expressed on this subject also reflect the varying historical perspectives of the individuals involved. Several respondents viewed the effects of radio and television on the storytelling tradition as a progressive, cumulative phenomenon—a collective "final blow." The comments of Liam Costello, Seán McDermot, and Peter Kelleher are illustrative of this, and revealing. Liam Costello is a former full-time folklore collector, now living in Galway city, and Seán McDermot is well known as a narrator of stories in Irish, living in Inveran, Co. Galway. Seán and Liam perceive the decline of storytelling in the context of nightly visiting to have begun with the coming of the bicycle and to have climaxed with the arrival of radio and television. According to Seán, Ireland began to improve slightly economically after World War I. In the 1920s, road works began on a larger scale; more construction was undertaken and more employment was available. People generally had a little more money to spend, and more bicycles began to appear in the countryside. With the bicycle came increased mobility, and many younger people began leaving their own villages for entertainment farther afield. These social developments resulted in a decrease in the importance of the domestic custom of *ar cuairt* for diversion and entertainment. The situation, as far as storytelling was concerned, was worsened by the introduction of the radio and television into Irish homes.

Liam Costello (Liam MacCoisdeala) worked in Galway as a full-time collector for the Irish Folklore Commission from 1936 to 1939. Liam recorded a great deal of material in the *Gaeltacht* area of Carna, a locality long well known for the richness of its storytelling tradition. Liam concurs with Seán that the introduction of the bicycle was one of the main factors in the decline of the storytelling tradition, and for the same reasons: the bicycle gave people more mobility and made it possible for them to seek out other forms of entertainment.[10] Such mobility was further increased by the appearance of the bus and the automobile; with these developments, other, more "exotic" forms of entertainment made their appearance in the countryside, particularly films and dance halls for "foreign" dancing. (Irish traditional dancing was done almost exclusively in people's homes, at least at night. It was conducted in the open air when weather conditions permitted.) These other diversions resulted in a further loss of interest in the storytelling tradition, particularly among young people, and, perhaps more important, a decreasing desire to learn the stories.

In regard to Carna, Costello agrees that the introduction of radio and television was more a *coup de coude*, a "nudge," than the *coup de grâce* in the decline of the tradition because the popularity of storytelling as a form of entertainment had already begun to decrease by the time the radio appeared. According to Costello, it was usually only the more sophisticated members of the community who possessed a radio set at that time (in the 1920s), an opinion which was confirmed by almost everyone to whom I spoke. Radios were by no means common in Irish households until perhaps the 1950s or later. In addition to these influences, Liam noted other social advances of this century—general progress in the standard of living and the greater availability of education—which combined to lessen the importance of storytelling in the life of the countryside.

An interesting corollary to the above comments are those of several individuals who live in *Gaeltacht* areas, or localities that were part of the *Gaeltacht* until quite recently. Máire Nic Aodha, Donal Moore, and Pappy McCarthy (of Na Cruacha, Co. Donegal; Ballinskelligs, Co. Kerry; and Gleninagh, Co. Clare, respectively) attributed the decline of storytelling in these areas to the large-scale depopulation caused by emigration, a process which had begun well before the arrival of the wireless and the later forms of technological advancement. The population in these areas of Donegal, Kerry, and Clare had decreased to the extent that there were simply very few people left to visit each other, let alone individuals with sufficient knowledge of the storytelling tradition to maintain and perpetuate it.[11]

The comments of Liam Costello and Seán McDermot provide a useful chronological framework for the body of commentary under discussion here. With the exception of emigration, all the factors influencing the visiting patterns and the concomitant changes in the contexts for storytelling have been placed within this century: from after World War I, as Seán suggests, to the present. Liam and Seán have experienced these changes within their lifetimes: Liam was collecting folklore in the 1930s; Seán was a teenager going *ar cuairt* in the 1920s. The comments of both pertain to areas of the country where Irish was the vernacular language. Peter Kelleher is a noted *uileann* ("elbow") pipe player whose involvement in the tradition has always been with storytelling in the English language. Peter has lived in Bullaun and Loughrea, in Co. Galway, which are within a few miles of each other. The radio began appearing in homes in the vicinity of Bullaun in the 1930s. In Peter's view, the coming of the radio into a household meant the disruption of normal conversation in that house because the attention of those present was focused on whatever program was being aired at the time. The storytelling which was a part of nightly visiting was thus disrupted, and the popularity of *ar cuairt* ultimately displaced, by this form of diversion. Peter felt that the arrival of television merely intensified a preexisting condition, but he added that, despite these developments, there were always a few homes in the area in which the old people who wanted to continued to gather and to entertain themselves in the ways to which they had been accustomed. In these contexts people still told the "old stories" until the individuals involved were no longer able to participate, primarily for reasons of illness or death. The passing of the old people who were the conservators of the storytelling tradition ended the visiting in the old style.[12]

Exclusive of radio and television, the availability of other forms of entertainment composes another significant category to which changes in the tradition are attributed. Jack Mahony discussed the influence of the phonograph in the area of Cloonfad, in Co. Roscommon. Jack's sister brought a "gramophone" home with her from America to Cloonfad in 1927. This was battery-operated and, at the time, one of only two phonographs within a fifty-mile radius of Jack's house. Jack regards this event as the beginning of the transition from storytelling to other modes of nightly entertainment, at least in his own home, for the neighbors then began to gather there in rather large numbers with the phonograph as the center of attention. The radio came somewhat later. (Jack acquired a radio in 1957.) Whatever the impact of the phonograph may have been in Cloonfad and its environs, Jack was the only person to attribute such importance to it.[13]

Dance Halls and Public Houses

So accustomed have we become to viewing mentally the context of rural storytelling around the "warm glow of the fireside" that it is easy to forget the often bitterly cold weather conditions that faced people during the wintertime and that either kept them at home or prevented them from traveling very far. Likewise, it is easy now, with the dramatic economic advances of recent decades, to overlook the social isolation and lack of stimulation country people must have experienced at times in the fairly recent past. A great deal has been written on the subject of the oppressive quality of life in rural Ireland and the serious depression attributed to Irish country people in the period between 1940 and the economic revival of the 1960s.[14] Such was the inaccessibility of some rural households in the first half of this century that, under the original plans of the Rural Electrification Scheme (implemented in 1947), fourteen percent of all rural dwellings were considered "so remote as to be outside the scope of any practical electrification scheme."[15] In *Folktales of Ireland* Richard Dorson gives us some idea of this isolation as recently as 1951:

> As we drove into the hills in our hired car, Tadhg [Murphy; collector for the Irish Folklore Commission] casually pointed to a little yellow building set like a flyspeck in the midst of empty stretching bogs and high ranges....Not another sign of life met the eye as one looked to the horizons, but in the morning barefooted children trooped from lonely farms for miles to converge

on that spot. Nine miles over a dirt road brought us to the mountainside dwelling where William (Liam) Stack [storyteller] had lived every day of his eighty years.[16]

It is not surprising that the increasing availability of various modes of transportation during this century drew ever-greater numbers of young people from their homes at night to attend the "extra domestic" forms of entertainment that were gaining in popularity in the countryside.

Dance halls and public houses ("pubs") also became important social outlets and were significant factors in the changing social networks of the agrarian population (see Table 1).[17] The appearance of large dance halls in country towns and outlying areas and the increasing importance of public houses in the social life of towns are both relatively recent developments.[18] The dance halls had attained their popularity by the 1960s. The entertainment they provided usually consisted of the kinds of music played by *ceili* bands, some jazz-style dance bands, and, considerably later, Irish "showbands." *Ceili* bands play mainly "old-fashioned" waltzes and traditional music but, occasionally, some country and western and "pop" music. The music of the showbands, which is influenced by British and American rock and roll, is decidedly more contemporary in sound, consisting of tunes, from whatever genres (including country music, sentimental ballads, and rock and roll) that are current "hits." *Ceili* bands and showbands are both still very popular in Ireland, although they appeal to somewhat different segments of the population.[19]

The tremendous resurgence of Irish traditional music, which began in the 1960s and shows no signs of abating, has had several important effects on the social life of the countryside. First, it is one of the main factors in the shift from the domestic performance of traditional music to the more public context of the pub. In fact, the playing of music of all kinds in pubs, on the scale and regularity with which it is now done in Ireland, is a new dimension in country life. Second, although it is only one of many factors, the bringing of entertainment into many of the pubs has been influential in both attracting women to public houses and, just as important, making their presence there more socially acceptable. Irish pubs, especially those in rural areas, have been overwhelmingly male sanctuaries until very recently; there are still many pubs in which a woman alone would be completely unwelcome.[20] The musical entertainment that many pubs now provide has been an enticement away from home for those of both sexes, particularly the young.

A noteworthy example of the potentially far-reaching effects of the establishment of a public house in a comparatively isolated community is that of Dunquin, Co. Kerry, which is an Irish speaking area on the very tip of the Dingle Peninsula. Cáit O'Sullivan (a narrator of stories in Irish, living in Dunquin) described the results of the opening of Maurice Kavanagh's pub, which is referred to as "Kruger's," in the early 1960s.[21] Prior to the establishment of "Kruger's," visiting among the neighbors was the only form of entertainment available. (There are still very few television sets in the general vicinity of Dunquin, as the reception there is very poor.) After Kruger's received its license, many of the men began frequenting the pub in the evenings for a drink and conversation. This virtually stopped the customary visiting. The opening of Kruger's, which is still the only pub in Dunquin, also altered some of the customs associated with funerals. In the past when someone died, those coming into Dunquin from neighboring towns and villages would gather at the home of the deceased person's relatives to wait for the funeral to begin. Now, these outsiders go directly to Kruger's. Thus two significant contexts for conversation and storytelling have been dramatically altered by the establishment of the one pub in the community.

Worthy of mention here also are Patrick O'Farrell's views on the deleterious effect he considers women to have had on the custom of nightly visiting and attendant storytelling. Patrick is a traditional musician who frequently plays in pubs in the area of Mullaghbawn, Co. Armagh, where he lives. According to Patrick, in the past it was customary for a husband and wife to keep family matters to themselves when socializing unless the situation warranted otherwise. Now, modern young women, both at home and in public (in pubs and various social gatherings), want more sophisticated entertainment, such as television, and they are more inclined to discuss such domestic matters as babies, children, and household problems. In general, they have intruded more private concerns into the normal contexts for storytelling, in which formerly they were not considered appropriate. Although the increasing presence of women in pubs is a subject upon which opinion was quite mixed,[22] Patrick's views on this aspect of the role of women in the storytelling tradition are completely idiosyncratic.

The Introduction of the Automobile

The automobile has been a factor in the decline of visiting customs for obvious reasons: it was one of the modes of transportation, among many, that opened up the farm or village to the enticements of the outside world.[23] But it had other, more subtle effects on storytelling as well. John Campbell felt that the very presence of the automobile introduced a new degree of impersonality into Irish life. Even today visitors to Ireland are often surprised at the friendliness of country people. It is customary to acknowledge someone coming toward you or passing by you on the road, even in a car.[24] In the past, when most people walked or rode bicycles, it was usual when people met for them to go at least part, if not the whole distance, together. In this way they would "shorten the road" for each other through the exchange of news and gossip, and the telling of stories. The use of the automobile decreases the amount of time required to reach one's destination and the frequency and likelihood of such chance encounters, in which storytelling might occur.

The increasing presence of the automobile has also affected the genesis of certain categories of stories. Dark country roads, fields, or dwellings were often the settings for extraordinary experiences that were ultimately expressed in narrative form, such as accounts of "going astray," hearing the *bean sídhe* or fairy music, or seeing apparitions of some kind (all typical *seanchas*). According to Francie Kennelly, people are no longer out on the roads at night as long as they were formerly, and the speed of travel in a car makes it much less likely that people will "see" the kinds of things they did in the past.[25]

Also affecting the generation of stories about supranormal experiences is the decline of the traditional wake in the face of the incipient acceptance of mortuaries in the countryside. A mortuary was constructed and opened in Miltown Malbay, where Mr. Kennelly lives, in the early 1980s.[26] Because there are now fewer wakes in the area, there is less travel to and from wake houses and less sitting up with the corpse. Consequently, fewer stories are being told about the strange happenings that seemed to thrive in these settings in the past (e.g., corpses sitting up, mourners hearing strange knocks or noises).[27]

The Modernization of Homes

The modernization of Irish homes also has influenced the decline of the tradition in a number of ways. Éamonn Ó Donnghaile, of Carna, Co. Galway, elaborated on the effect that the transition from open fireplaces to turf-burning stoves in country kitchens had on those who enjoyed visiting and telling stories. The customary place for family and visitors to gather was in the kitchen around the fireplace. In the recent past, the floors in Irish homes were concrete. When Éamonn was in his twenties (he is now in his late fifties), linoleum began to be used to cover the concrete floors. Then, about thirty-five years ago, the open fireplaces gave way to turf-burning stoves, which were completely enclosed. According to Éamonn, the first stoves of this kind were black and did not require much care. But when white stoves were introduced, they required a good deal more upkeep, and women subsequently became much more house proud.[28] It had been the general practice for male visitors who were smokers or tobacco chewers to spit into the open fireplaces; this was no longer possible with the turf stoves, and the women began discouraging such visitors. The ceiliers of the locality were reluctant to give up the comfort they had known, and they began to seek out houses where they could still feel at ease until, as Éamonn put it, "the last house fell to modernization."

Another subtle effect that the modernization of homes has had on the storytelling tradition has been brought about by the substitution of the full door (single piece) for the "Dutch door" or "half door." In many of the older cottages the main and only entrance to the house was the kitchen door, which was composed of two parts, top and bottom ("half doors"), which could be opened or closed independently. John Campbell noted that the top half of the door was always kept open, which allowed for greetings and conversation and often the telling of stories. John pointed out to me that this was possible because these cottages, with no other door and few if any windows, had no cross-ventilation. The cold air from outside did not come in because the air could not circulate. Houses in the newer style, though, which no longer have the half doors, and where the entry way is often separate from the other rooms of the house, are not as open—physically or psychologically—as houses were in the past.[29] A different system of ventilation makes it impossible to leave doors open in the cold winter weather, and this internal orientation of the household cuts off its inhabitants, to some degree, from passersby ("the outside world"). The newer houses, therefore, even with more windows and allowing more light, actually have less permeable psychological boundaries.[30]

Education, Literacy, and the Decline of the Language

Our final considerations here are those of education, newspapers, and the decline of the Irish language. By and large, "education and newspapers" were suggested as part of the larger picture of social change and were not usually isolated as primary causes of the changes in rural customs. However, they were given prominence in my conversations with Pappy McCarthy and Tomás Laighléis, who offered some interesting views on these subjects. Pappy regarded television, radio, and the newspapers as collectively responsible for the decline in the storytelling tradition. These three forms of communication made country people more aware of the outside world and of the ways people lived in other countries. Because of this exposure to other possibilities, they became more dissatisfied with Irish country life. Pappy felt that this dissatisfaction was only worsened by the tourists coming into the country and telling Irish people that they were "behind the times." Because young people felt a desire to "keep up with the times," they turned to more modern forms of entertainment.

Although Pappy did not specifically mention the importance of returning immigrants during our discussion, they are implied here; returning immigrants have always had considerable influence on family members and friends who remained behind in the countryside. In the late 1940s, when emigration from the Irish countryside had reached near-crisis levels, the government appointed a commission to look into the problem. The report on the commission's findings, published in 1956, presented statistics on the lack of sanitary facilities on the Irish farms of the time. The report stated, "through the cinema and the radio, and above all by direct experience either personal or through relatives, people in such conditions are, more than ever before, becoming aware of the contrast between their way of life and that in other countries, especially in urban centres."[31]

Tomás Laighléis, of Menlo, Co. Galway, was nearly ninety years of age at the time that I interviewed him, and he had some very interesting perceptions of the causes of the changes that occurred in the storytelling tradition in the locality. Tomás earmarked the period of 1916-1922, beginning with the Easter Rising in 1916, as the turning point for the tradition of oral narration. In the early part of this century, this locality was completely Irish speaking, and the general level of formal education was such that few individuals could either read or write the Irish language. The Rising generated a desire for greater education in a very concrete fashion. Because there were no newspapers in Menlo itself at the time, the only information available during the week following the rebellion was that which circulated as rumor. The years between the Rising and the Civil War of 1921-1922 were ones of great social upheaval, and the need for information about national events stimulated the desire to learn to read (i.e., to read English). Mr. Laighléis underscores the pivotal role of the Rebellion in this process in the following anecdote:[32]

CH: What makes you pin it down to that—that period now?
TL: Now, 19—Because, I'll tell you, now, why the time of the Rising. That was in '16. 1916.
CH: Yes. Yeah, right. "Easter"? Yeah.
TL: And, I remember well, on account of the Rising, there was nothing going but rumors because there was no paper going at the time, on account of the Rising. But, nevertheless, the Connacht radio in Galway gave out a supplement...[unintelligible])...on some day [?] during the week. On Saturday—Friday and Saturday—Or Saturday, they used to come out with it as a da—as a weekly paper. But, I was coming down from the fields this

day, and there was—it was raining. And there was a few more with me. And we started talking about this and that; about the rumors were a-going around that such a place was blown up or, or a bridge was slapped. There was no much—not much talk about it [?]. Bombin' that fella, blowing up them, knocking them down good [?]. And, when we came to the crossroads there above the Galway road, and when we, we..[unintelligible]...an old car [cart] from town. They used to—Every woman used to go to town that time with milk [for cooperative creameries]. And, I asked her—oh, she knew us well—if she—had she any news. "I have the paper here with me," she said. And even though it was raining, he—she had the paper in the car. She shooks it out then. We covered ourselves well with the old bags. Not with overcoats at all, but the old bags we had. And, we started it. I look— looked at the heading. 'Twas I who got it. Well, I was the best of them reading. Sure, I could read. But, nevertheless, I remember the headings yet, "Alleged General Rising in Ireland." That was the heading. And every one of them wanted to have a peep at the paper; avail themselves...[unintelligible]...they had. But, we hadn't far to go to our house, and we were thankful. That was the first real indication we had that—that the Rebellion was gone. It was only rumor until then.

CH: So that started...
TL: From that on I...Every lad got interested in papers and in better reading, and they started.
CH: That makes a lot of sense. Yeah.
TL: And, from that on, the storytelling fell back.

As Mr. Laighléis views it, once people started learning to read, they turned to the stories in the newspapers and other printed sources for their entertainment. Many of these stories were folktales, and it became more common for those who were literate to recite such stories to those who were not. These events increased the reliance on printed versions of stories, and thereby decreased the importance of the tradition of oral storytelling in the local community.[33]

In presenting the changes in the storytelling tradition in the context of national events and the growth of literacy, Mr. Laighléis has hinted at two very important issues. First, as ironic as it seems, the growth of literacy in English was a crucial prerequisite for the development of Irish nationalism on a broad cultural scale, a dovetailing of which Mr. Laighléis seems aware. Second, as Martin Waters points out, increased literacy made it possible for large numbers of Irish people, through political propaganda and the historical romances published in the popular press, to acquaint themselves with a version of Ireland's past that was recast in a nationalistic mold.[34] As we know, the Irish Literary Revival was inextricably linked to the cause of Irish nationalism; stories about the Irish past, often based on the early saga material and nationalistic in their thrust, circulated in various literary media throughout the country in the early part of this century.

The parameter of the views presented above is the period from 1916 to the present. In fact, the times stipulated for the commencement of changes in the tradition are highly variable. The weight of opinion falls with radio and television as the primary causal factors but, as I noted, the chronological distribution and geographical distribution of radio and television sets in the countryside have been by no means uniform. The majority of the respondents place the date of the changes under discussion at intervals varying from twenty to forty years ago, which is actually quite recent. For Martin McKenna, who lives in Fanore, Co. Clare, this transition occurred even more recently. Television was introduced into the area about fifteen years before the time of my conversation with him. It was this event that eventually caused Martin to stop telling his stories, for television took preeminence over *ar cuairt* as a form of entertainment in Fanore relatively quickly. In addition, although everyone interviewed during the course of this research noted a decline in the custom of nightly visiting as it was carried on in the past, not everyone felt that it had ceased entirely. For Éamonn Ó Donnghaile in Carna, John Reilly in Dunmore, James Delaney in Athlone (Co. Westmeath), and John Campbell in Forkhill, it continues, although all concur that it is currently on a much more limited scale and on a more formal basis than before. This diversity of opinion indicates that the answers to these questions are not "objective facts" at all; they are reflections of regional development, personal experience, idiosyncratic viewpoints, and even a matter of definition.

The final influences I wish to discuss are relatively minor (in terms of frequency) and, strictly speaking, fall outside the category of "modernization." Some have already been noted in passing. In addition to the specific explanations offered for the changes in the storytelling tradition, there is the factor of the decline of the Irish language, a view expressed by folklore collector James Delaney.[35] Chronologically, this factor antedates and subsumes those parameters set above, for the decline of the language has literally been in progress for centuries. The coming of Christianity in the fifth century introduced a written culture to Ireland and, over the course of the centuries, Latin and English began to predominate in the formal spheres of culture and education. English had become the predominant language of the "professional classes" by the late sixteenth century. The decline in the Irish language has never lessened and has been most dramatic in the last two centuries.[36]

The situation regarding the decline of Irish Gaelic has been of tremendous importance in Irish folklore scholarship, particularly the study of the narrative tradition in English, because one of the basic assumptions of much of the research done in this area has been, and still is, that this corpus of narrative is merely the detritus of the tradition in Irish.[37] However, in my experience, the decline of the language, and scholarly assumptions about it, appear to have had little impact on those narrators whose entire experience has been with the English language tradition. This fact is significant in itself and raises important issues in terms of the research and scholarship undertaken in this field. For this reason I am reserving my discussion of the problem of the decline of the language for Chapter Three, which compares the status of the narrators in the two language traditions.

The "Death" of the Tradition

The storytelling tradition—at least the telling of long, structurally complex tales—is associated with the past, with old people, and with the previous generations of country people, despite the fact that such stories are still told by relatively young men such as John Campbell. On several occasions responses to my questions about the causes of changes in the tradition consisted of statements such as, "Oh, storytelling died out with the old people," or "Storytelling is a thing of the past." Because of my experiences on my 1981 visit to Ireland, I was accustomed to such formulations of the situation. What did surprise me were the few occasions on which the turning point for the narrative tradition consisted of just one person—at least in the perceptions of the person to whom I spoke. The narrating of *sean-sgéalta* disappeared from the areas of Galway and Roscommon in which John Reilly and Jack Mahony live (within a few miles of each other) with the death of John's father, who was the only local narrator of stories of this kind. Tom Donohoe, a man to whom I spoke in Gleninagh, Co. Clare, and a native Irish speaker, had learned one story from Martin Nestor, who, as I noted previously, was well known for his storytelling in the village. Tom noted that after Martin's death in 1947 "there was no one telling stories." The final example is that of Máire Nic Aodha, who lives in an extremely sparsely settled area of Donegal which is still completely Irish speaking. Máire is highly regarded as a teller of the old tales by the now-retired Donegal collector, Seán Ó hEochaidh.[38] (Seán had been a full time collector for forty-eight years.) Máire concluded our discussion of the factors influencing the tradition in the locality with this comment: "When Seán Ó hEochaidh left this place, I think the old stories went with Seán. I think they went with Seán now." No other statement I have encountered so aptly encapsulates the importance of the activities of folklore collectors to the storytelling tradition in both languages, a subject to which I return in Chapter Two.

The implications of the influence of modernization have been presented here from the points of view of the individuals involved in this study. These comments range from broad statements about technological innovations of which we are all aware to opinions that reveal subtle variations in personal experience and insight. The majority of variables have been placed well within this century. The next subject to be considered is that of the overall influence that folklore collecting in Ireland has had on the storytelling tradition in the past and continues to have in its perpetuation.

Notes to Chapter One

1. I have not included any of the comments of the nine people I interviewed in Muckross and Killarney, Co. Kerry, because I was unable to locate any traditional storytellers in these localities.

2. J. E. Caerwyn Williams points this out in the "Introduction" to *The Irish Storyteller and His Tales* (Patrick K. Ford, unpublished translation, p. 56). J. E. Caerwyn Williams, *Y Storïwr Gwyddeleg a'i Chwedlau* (Cardiff: University of Wales Press, 1972). In the many works I have checked in which the word "peasant" is used, either in the title or in the body of the work, it is rarely defined. Its generally accepted meaning is "someone who tills the soil as a small landowner or worker," and that is the way in which I use it here. It is worth noting in the Irish context, however, that this "peasantry" was by no means a completely homogeneous group, and its members were quite aware of the complex distinctions made within it. See S. J. Connolly, *Priests and People in Pre-Famine Ireland, 1780-1845*, (Dublin: Gill and Macmillan, 1982), p. 55.

3. Paul Johnson, *Ireland: A Concise History from the Twelfth Century to the Present Day* (London: Granada, 1981), p. 97.

4. Michael J. Shiel, *The Quiet Revolution* (Dublin: The O'Brien Press, 1984), pp. 112-13.

5. Kenneth Neill, *The Irish People: An Illustrated History* (New York: Mayflower Books, 1979), p. 220. Actually, Ireland's economic base began improving at the beginning of this century. For a brief discussion of this see Johnson, *Ireland: A Concise History*, p. 155. For a more detailed discussion of the economic revival of the 1960s, see Terence Brown, *Ireland : A Social and Cultural History, 1922-79* (Glasgow: Fontana, 1981), pp. 241-266.

6. Although in Irish *ar cuairt* is grammatically a prepositional phrase, it is often used in English as a noun, as I use it here.

7. Henry Glassie, *Passing the Time in Ballymenone: Culture and History of an Ulster Community* (Philadelphia: University of Pennsylvania Press, 1982), p. 487.

8. The geographical province of Ulster consists of nine counties, three of which are part of the Republic of Ireland: Donegal, Cavan, and Monaghan. The other counties are Londonderry, Antrim, Tyrone, Down, Armagh, and Fermanagh, which constitute Northern Ireland. Connacht includes counties Galway, Clare, Leitrim, Roscommon, Mayo, and Sligo. In Ireland one pays an annual fee for a license to use a television set or a radio. There is much pirating, as one would expect, and this figure is based on the number of people who actually obeyed the law. See Brown, *Ireland: A Social and Cultural History*, p. 153, for further discussion of these statistics.

9. In the statistics Shiel provides on the ownership of domestic appliances, eighty-four percent of rural electricity consumers possessed television sets in 1979. No doubt this percentage has increased considerably in the intervening years. Shiel, *The Quiet Revolution*, pp. 164-66.

10. Vivian Mercier (personal communication, March 29, 1987) informed me that his maternal grandfather, David Abbott, D. D. (Archdeacon of Clogher, Church of Ireland, d. 1917), had said that the bicycle had changed Irish rural life more than any other factor in his lifetime. Abbott had served in rural parishes in Monaghan and Armagh for about forty years.

11. Na Cruacha, which is still all Irish speaking, is a very remote and isolated spot at the base of the Bluestack Mountains in Co. Donegal. Only a handful of houses, at considerable distance from each other, remain in the locality. In *Irish Life and Lore* (Dublin and Cork: The Mercier Press, 1982), p. 53, Séamas Ó Catháin describes thus an area of the Bluestacks, in Donegal, which he had visited often: "....for this once populous valley...where wooden bridges once resounded to the clatter of dancing feet at Sunday evening dances, is now almost totally denuded of its people."

12. This view was also expressed by Seán Ó Flannagáin of Killgalligan, Co. Mayo, an excellent narrator of stories in Irish.

13. The phonograph (or "gramophone") does not appear in Shiel's list of domestic appliances owned by rural electricity consumers (figures provided for the period 1958-79), suggesting it may have had little impact on the countryside as a whole. See Shiel, *The Quiet Revolution*, p. 166.

14. For an astute, if somewhat brief, overview of the received wisdom and more controversial evaluations of this period, see Brown, *Ireland: A Social and Cultural History*, pp. 182-98.

15. Shiel, *The Quiet Revolution*, p. 250.

16. Richard M. Dorson, "Foreword" to *Folktales of Ireland*, ed. Sean O'Sullivan (Chicago: University of Chicago Press, 1966), p. xxix.

17. "Various Entertainments" is a category in which I have listed the number of respondents who provided multiple answers about forms of entertainment with more or less equal weight.

18. The implementation of the Rural Electrification Scheme facilitated social activities in the countryside, including public dances. See Shiel, *The Quiet Revolution*, pp. 8-10. The emergence of the dance halls was not without its detractors, particularly among the clergy, some of whom perceived such close proximity for young people of both sexes as sources of "temptation" and possible "occasions of sin." As Martin J. Waters notes of the "mixed" Irish classes offered by the Gaelic League, "Given the puritanical mentality of the Irish clergy, these opportunities for sociability between the sexes could be very disturbing indeed...." Martin J. Waters, "Peasants and Emigrants: Considerations of the Gaelic League as a Social Movement," in *Views of the Irish Peasantry*, ed. Daniel J. Casey and Robert E. Rhodes (Hamden, Conn.: Archon Books, 1977), p. 171.

19. The *ceili* bands tend to be popular in the countryside and in the smaller towns, and also to be popular with older people. The showbands are a more urban phenomenon, and are very popular in the dance halls in Dublin. They are also a welcome attraction in the dance halls around the country. Many Irish showbands command large audiences in England and the United States. There are also differences of instrumentation, but they are not relevant here.

20. I have experienced this myself on a number of occasions. Nothing might be said, but the message is unmistakable. The modern trend is for pubs to have a "bar" on one side, and a "lounge" on the other. Conventionally, couples and women alone are expected to go into the lounge; women usually do not go into the bar.

21. Mrs. O'Sullivan was uncertain of the year. "Kruger's" is actually known all over Ireland because Dunquin is a recognized beauty spot. Many tourists, Irish and otherwise, travel through it during the summer or come to spend their holidays there; people also come to Dunquin to learn or improve their Irish.

22. For example, Tomás Laighléis of Menlo, Co. Galway, shared Mr. O'Farrell's negative view of the presence of women in pubs. Tomás disliked seeing women in pubs because he felt it made them look "masculine." The sexes have been kept apart in Ireland to an enormous degree until very recently. No doubt, this is what Mr. O'Farrell is actually reacting to. For a brief discussion of the changing status of Irish women during the last century see Ruth Dudley Edwards, *An Atlas of Irish History* (London: Methuen and Co., 1973; reprint ed., London and New York: Methuen and Co., 1981), pp. 247-49. Tomás Laighléis' recollections of the history of Menlo, Co. Galway, were edited by Tomás de Bhaldraithe and published as *Seanchas Thomáis Laighléis* (Baile Átha Cliath: An Clóchomhar Tta., 1977).

23. In *Passing the Time in Ballymenone*, p. 605, Henry Glassie poetically points out that the increasing number of automobiles and roads has resulted in a shift in orientation for both the homes and the community of Ballymenone (Co. Fermanagh). At one time, "a network of paths tied scattered habitations into the community's own center. Now houses are pulled to the thoroughfares and pointed at the larger world."

24. Whatever the mode of transportation in use, I have rarely, if ever, not been greeted in some fashion when I encountered someone on the road in Ireland.

25. Mr. Kennelly informed me that it used to take six hours to travel from Miltown Malbay to Ennis (Co. Clare) by horse and cart, which is a distance of less than twenty miles.

26. It was built in the interval between my 1981 and 1983 visits to Ireland. This is the only mortuary that I have seen in a country town, but because there was no outward indication of the nature of the business carried on within, I may simply not have noticed them in other places. In this instance, the door was open when I passed by, through which I saw (much to my surprise) a corpse laid out—and facing me—in a coffin.

27. There are many stories in Irish tradition about pranks and rather farcical happenings at wakes. For a full treatment of traditional customs at Irish wakes of the past, see Seán Ó Súilleabháin, *Irish Wake Amusements* (Dublin and Cork: The Mercier Press, 1967). There is considerable difference of opinion among the individuals interviewed for this study as to the actual *decline* of the wake. Martin McKenna, for example, stated that the wake had basically disappeared in Murrough, Co. Clare, where he lives. According to John Campbell, wakes are still being held in Forkhill, Co. Armagh, and this is one of the contexts in which he hears new stories to add to his repertoire. Éamonn Ó Donnghaile, in Carna, Co. Galway, is still expected to tell stories at wakes. The divergence of opinion seems to reflect differences in personal experience and regional variations in the customs associated with wakes.

28. The turf stoves I have seen are actually more off-white or very light tan in color rather than stark white.

29. John Campbell is a particularly personable man. He loves conversation and loves to talk and seems, in general, to be exceptionally sensitive to the nuances of social arrangements. The concluding sentence of Lawrence Millman's book on Ireland, *Our Like Will Not Be There Again*, p. 209, supports John's comments on this matter. It states that "the Blasket people always leave their doors open." Lawrence Millman, *Our Like Will Not Be There Again* (Boston: Little, Brown & Co., 1977).

30. Henry Glassie points out that in Ballymenone the terrain has shifted in the direction of growing individualism. He states: "From a landscape crowded with hamlets and little farms, to a landscape of private homes and big farms, the depopulated lands shift to provide privacy and enable individual success." Glassie, *Passing the Time in Ballymenone*, p. 604.

31. *Commission on Emigration, 1948-1954*, p. 174, quoted in Brown, *Ireland: A Social and Cultural History*, p. 184.

32. Although the point of Tomás' anecdote is clear—that there was a connection between political events and an increase in the desire for literacy—it is unclear here whether or not Menlo had any radio communication with Dublin at this time.

33. Mr. Laighléis' views on the situation that developed in Menlo actually recapitulate a problem with which Irish folklore scholars have always been concerned: the interplay of oral and written versions of traditional material. Written versions of folktales have appeared in popular publications, such as *Ireland's Own*, and through the process of recital, have been taken into oral tradition; stories from oral tradition have also appeared in such publications. For a discussion of these concerns, see "Ireland's Own" in Séamas Ó Catháin's *The Bedside Book of Irish Folklore* (Dublin and Cork: The Mercier Press, 1980), pp. 11-16. For a more scholarly treatment of this issue, see Seán Ó Coileáin, "Oral vs. Literary? Some Strands of the Argument," *Studia Hibernica* 17-18 (1977-78): 7-35. An interesting discussion of the different organs in which a folktale may be found, and in varying degrees of bowdlerization, appears in James MacKillop's discussion of the "Legend of Knockmany." See James MacKillop, "Finn Mac Cool: The Hero and the Anti-Hero in Irish Folk Tradition," in *Views of the Irish Peasantry*, ed. Daniel J. Casey and Robert E. Rhodes (Hamden, Conn.: Archon Books, 1977), pp. 100-105.

34. Waters, p. 165.

35. It is a view held by many scholars. For example, in his study of the Irish narrative tradition, J. E. Caerwyn Williams avers that "the storytelling tradition was itself bound up with the language." Williams [Ford], p. 40.

36. Edwards, *An Atlas of Irish History*, pp. 244-247. Edwards points out that in 1851 only 25% of the population spoke Irish; by 1911, only 12%. Although some improvement has been made because of the compulsory teaching of Irish, it is not statistically significant.

37. Williams states the following in regard to narratives in the English language: "It is true that many English language tales have been collected in...those areas from which Irish has disappeared, but from the standpoint of number, quality, and art, they cannot be compared with Irish tales." Williams [Ford], p. 40. Delargy makes a comparable statement in "The Gaelic Story-Teller": "Both the international as well as the native *märchen* are more generally to be found in Irish than in English, and although many folk-tales of this kind have been recorded in English, the Anglo-Irish wonder-tale of the international type compares very unfavorably both as to style and content with similar tales in Irish." Delargy, pp. 180-81.

38. Some of Máire's husband's tales appear in Seán Ó hEochaidh's collection of fairy legends, *Siscéalta Ó Thír Chonaill*, trans. Máire MacNeill; ed. Séamas Ó Catháin (Dublin: Comhairle Bhéaloideas Éireann, 1977), pp. 280-85.

2

FOLKLORE COLLECTORS AND THE IRISH STORYTELLING TRADITION

THE PIVOTAL ROLE OF THE COLLECTORS
Collecting in the Past

As I have stated previously, the goal of those engaged in folklore research in Ireland on a professional basis has always been the collection, documentation, and preservation of those materials considered to be the best examples of survivals from the old, "peasant" life.[1] At the time that the documentation of the tradition began under the auspices of the Irish government, the storytelling tradition was considered to be in decline. For recording purposes the folklore collectors sought out those individuals regarded in their localities as the remaining masters of their craft, whose narratives would be representative examples, for posterity, of the linguistic elegance and dexterity achieved by the "unlettered" storytellers of the past. As the collectors traversed their respective areas, they also found many persons with varying degrees of knowledge of, and participation in, the storytelling tradition. Among these were individuals whom Swedish folklorist von Sydow terms "passive bearers" of tradition: individuals who were familiar with the stories told locally, but who themselves never took on the role of narrator, or others who had forgotten, through infrequency of narration or other causes, the stories they had told in the past.[2] They also found many who were active but less talented narrators.

The available documentation of the activities of the early collectors, including Séamus Ó Duilearga (James Delargy), indicates how important the interest of these fieldworkers was in motivating some of those who had ceased to tell their stories to work them up for the collectors and, on occasion, even to become active storytellers again. In "The Gaelic Story-Teller," Ó Duilearga discusses the impact of his collecting activities on several such passive bearers of tradition. When Ó Duilearga was recording material in Co. Clare during the 1940s, he made an appointment with one Seán Carún, who lived in the area of Doolin. When Ó Duilearga arrived for this meeting, Carún was not to be found anywhere. He eventually returned, quite late. Several months later Ó Duilearga learned from Carún's wife the reason for his absence:

>...when he was not to be found, he had gone into a cave in the mountain above his house to wrestle with his memory, striving to recall tales which he had heard...some forty years before, and which he had forgotten: he had returned in triumph with three of these tales restored to their home in his memory....[3]

Another notable example is Stiofán Ó hEalaoire, also of Co. Clare. Ó Duilearga reports that Ó hEalaoire was unknown to his neighbors as a storyteller until after Ó Duilearga had recorded dozens of well-rendered narratives from him. He was subsequently "much sought after as a storyteller."[4] Thus, although the ideal of the collectors was to find excellent narrators, they also found and recorded storytellers of greatly varying ability, and their endeavors occasionally resulted in the bringing of latent master narrators, such as Ó hEalaoire, to the fore. For many, it was the first real attention that anyone had paid to their stories and their narrative skills in quite some time, and they were more than anxious to recount their tales for the collectors.[5]

Folklore Collecting Today

My own experiences as a fieldworker in Ireland in the 1980s among traditional narrators reveal that, in many ways, the situation has not changed all that dramatically over the intervening years. Despite the activities of collectors, or perhaps because of them, there is no single, direct path to the accolade of "traditional storyteller," particularly for narrators in English. The ways in which the majority of the storytellers in English I interviewed came to have their stories recorded (prior to my research) were surprisingly happenstantial and had little to do with preexisting reputations as "storytellers." Only a few of the narrators attracted the attention of collectors because of any stature or reputation they had already achieved in their localities as storytellers.

Donal Moore is a case in point. Donal is a bilingual narrator living in Ballinskelligs, Co. Kerry, an area long noted for its tradition bearers. Séamus Ó Duilearga was first referred to Donal about twenty-five years ago, when he was collecting in the area. Donal has since been recorded by many other individuals interested in traditional storytelling. But Donal is primarily a narrator of stories in Irish; he began narrating in English in response to the interest shown in his stories by English speakers who could not understand Gaelic. John Campbell has a considerable reputation as a storyteller in Northern Ireland, but his experience of the tradition is atypical. He is usually paid for his performances, and his reputation has been affected by appearances on radio and television as well as performances in various public settings. (Since the time of my interviews with John, he has performed on several occasions at the International Storytelling Festival in London.) Indeed, almost all the storytellers I interviewed have been passive bearers of tradition. Martin McKenna and Packie Murrihy (both of Co. Clare), for instance, were known among some of the people of their localities for having "the old stories," but both were recorded sometime after the decline of the tradition of nightly visiting and when they had far fewer opportunities to tell their stories in normal social settings. By the time Tom Munnelly came to see Martin McKenna in the 1970s he had forgotten most of his stories and had virtually ceased narrating. Mr. Murrihy recounted some of the longest and most complex tales that I recorded, but Mr. Munnelly was the first to record any of his stories, and at a time when Packie was already in his seventies and quite infirm.[6]

Based on the material recorded during my interviews, the experiences of the narrators in English with folklore collectors reveal two very interesting phenomena. First, for some the development of the self-concept of "storyteller" or the recognition of functioning in this role resulted from the experience of being recorded by a professional folklore collector. Second, the emergence of several individuals as "storytellers" is linked to their performance as traditional musicians. As we shall see in the experiences of some of the storytellers, these categories are not mutually exclusive.

In the first category we find Francie Kennelly, Frank Anderson, Patrick O'Farrell, and Elizabeth Bourke. Their recognition as "storytellers" is a comparatively recent development. They did not have previous reputations as narrators, and the ways in which the collectors learned that they knew some of the "old stories" were largely serendipitous. Francie Kennelly is an interesting example. He was recorded by collector Tom Munnelly about five years before my 1983 interview with him. Muiris Ó Rócháin, a schoolteacher living in Miltown Malbay, where Francie lives, met him at a wedding; in the course of their conversation Muiris learned that Francie knew some of the old stories. Mr. Ó Rócháin later conveyed this information to Mr. Munnelly, who contacted Francie. Since Mr. Munnelly began interviewing him, Francie has become more aware that these stories are valued by folklore collectors and those interested in traditional culture. He has also begun to think of himself as a *storyteller* and to put himself forward in this role when opportunities occur. Although he had never previously narrated in public, he has told several of his stories at one of the Willie Clancy Summer Schools in Miltown Malbay and joined John Campbell sometime later for a performance at the International Storytelling Festival in London.[7]

Frank Anderson is another noteworthy example. Frank is a traditional musician and singer. Bairbre Ó Floinn, collector and archivist for the Department of Irish Folklore at University College, Dublin, once heard Frank singing with a group of musicians in a pub in Ballinagare, Co. Roscommon. Bairbre subsequently made arrangements with Frank to record him, during which time she became aware that Frank also knew many stories about local happenings which involved traditional themes. As a result of his connections with Bairbre, Frank's music has been recorded for the archives of the Department of Irish Folklore as well as those of Trinity College (Dublin), and he has performed in several Dublin pubs noted for their traditional music. Some of Frank's songs were recorded during these sessions and later broadcast on the radio. This exposure eventually led to Frank's appearance on a television program with eleven other people from all over Ireland, telling fairy stories and other tales about local events. (The program's producers had contacted Bairbre Ó Floinn about potential participants.) For this television program Frank had consciously to refresh his memory concerning the stories that he knew about past events—stories he himself had never told before about events that had occurred more than forty years ago. Because of Frank's initial chance meeting with Bairbre, he was unexpectedly placed in the role of storyteller. The cumulative effect of all this is that Frank is now known in the area of Ballinagare as a personality of sorts, and local people are used to seeing him with folklorists (as I experienced personally). He is also consciously aware of himself in two roles: that of traditional musician, which he has always been, and that of storyteller, a more or less chance occurrence.

Patrick O'Farrell and Elizabeth Bourke have had similar experiences. Mr. O'Farrell was playing his accordion on one occasion in a pub in Mullaghbawn (Co. Armagh), when collector Michael J. Murphy came in.[8] They got into a conversation, and Mr. Murphy found out that Patrick knew a traditional story about "the Danes." Murphy later came to see Patrick and recorded this story from him.[9] Although Mr. O'Farrell knows a great deal about local history and traditional medicine, he is not an accomplished narrator; prior to this he had never really considered himself a storyteller. He subsequently appeared on an annual radio program in Northern Ireland for several years in succession discussing his ideas about history and his predictions for the future. Also, a woman from the United States came to record some local history from him. At the time that I met Mr. O'Farrell, which was quite by accident (I was hitchhiking from Forkhill to Dublin and he and his son offered me a ride), he seemed to have incorporated these additional experiences into his self-image, for he represented himself to me as a "storyteller."

Elizabeth Bourke's name was given to Séamas Ó Catháin of the Department of Irish Folklore by a teacher at the vocational school in Killala, Co. Mayo, when Ó Catháin was doing research in the area. Mrs. Bourke was subsequently recorded for the archives of the Department of Irish Folklore by Séamas Ó Catháin and Bairbre Ó Floinn. Mrs. Bourke had never previously regarded herself as a storyteller, nor had she ever told before any of the stories that were recorded by the collectors. She later appeared on the same program as Frank Anderson, telling stories about local occurrences. The attention that Mrs. Bourke has received for the kind of stories that she can tell seemed to have affected her life and her view of herself very little, perhaps because of her advanced age at the time all this occurred. (She was almost ninety at the time that I spoke to her in 1984.)

The other process I observed involves those individuals who emerged as "storytellers" because of the attention they initially received for their musicianship. Frank Anderson, whose experiences are discussed above, falls into this category. (Patrick O'Farrell does also, but more coincidentally, for he just happened to be playing music in the situation in which Michael Murphy met him; their acquaintance was not because of it.) The others are Martin ("Junior") Crehan, Catherine Droney, Peter Kelleher, and, again indirectly, John Reilly. Junior is a well known traditional musician in west Clare, and his name was originally given to me by Tom Munnelly. Junior has been involved in traditional music as a fiddle player all his life and had developed a reputation locally as such when Tom, a specialist in traditional music, began working in Clare in the late 1970s. Through the process of recording Junior's music, Tom became aware that Junior could tell some of the old stories, and he recorded several of them. The same is true of Catherine Droney, who was well known for her traditional singing in both Irish and English. Mrs. Droney lived in Clare, and Tom Munnelly became aware of the kinds of stories Mrs. Droney knew in the course of recording her songs. (Mrs. Droney died several years ago.[10]) Mr. Munnelly's acquaintanceship with John Reilly is indirectly related to John's interest in traditional music. Tom met John at the house of a woman in Roscommon (Jack Mahony's neighbor) who was a traditional singer.[11] (Although based in Co. Clare,

Tom records many kinds of traditional material all over Ireland in his capacity as collector for the Department of Irish Folklore in Dublin.)

The degree to which these individuals have taken on the role of "storyteller" varies, but it is to a much lesser degree than either Frank Anderson or Patrick O'Farrell. Junior's primary identity is clearly that of musician. Although he thinks of himself as "knowing" the old stories, this is less important to him than performing as a musician, which he still does regularly in the area around Miltown Malbay. The contexts in which Junior often plays—pubs that offer traditional music—are not settings that allow for the telling of long, traditional tales, music being the main attraction. However, Junior is willing to put himself forward as an active bearer of the tradition in less public settings, such as in his own home or for collectors. At the time that I met Catherine Droney, she was in her eighties, and Tom Munnelly had been recording material from her during the eight years she had lived in Ballyvaughan (Co. Clare). Mrs. Droney was still willing to perform publicly as a traditional singer, but she had never told any of her stories outside her home. There was obviously a personal reticence on her part about doing so, in which her age may have played a substantial part. She might have developed this part of her identity in some way if she had been a younger woman when her relationship with folklore collectors developed. John Reilly presents a very particular problem because he is an intensely shy man. Although a superb narrator of *seanchas*, he does not seem willing to play *any* public role. Whether or not this presents a problem for John as far as his storytelling is concerned is difficult to determine because there is now so little narrating of the kinds of stories John knows in the area in which he lives (Dunmore, Co. Galway).[12]

Peter Kelleher is the only one of this group whose self-image as "storyteller" has developed independently of the interest that folklore collectors have shown in his stories. Peter is a traditional musician (*uilleann* ["elbow"] pipes and concert flute); he has performed with the Athenry Mummers and toured England with *Comhaltas Ceoltóirí Éireann* ("Brotherhood of Irish Musicians") groups. Peter started telling jokes and shorter "yarns" during these performances, and over time the demand for his stories increased. Because he is now expected to tell stories in such settings, he actively expands his repertoire. Although Peter has been recorded for several radio programs on local history and people come to see him from all over the world for information about traditional music, no one interested in storytelling per se had ever contacted him before our conversations.

A question suggested by the foregoing examples is surely this: What makes it possible for individuals with differing capabilities as narrators and experience of the tradition to step so easily—almost casually—into the role of "storyteller"? The answer to this question, based upon the individuals involved in this study, seems to entail three related factors: the relationship between the activities of folklore collectors and the dynamics of the tradition itself; the self-consciousness of the tradition; and the gap between popular conceptions of traditional storytelling and the reality of that tradition.

Self-Consciousness and the Storytelling Tradition

In the course of conducting this research I was, to some extent, following paths trodden by previous collectors, primarily Mr. Munnelly and Bairbre Ó Floinn, who put me in touch with the majority of the narrators of stories in English. Seven of the fifteen storytellers whose tales are presented in my doctoral dissertation live in County Clare, a group which also includes most of the narrators of the long, multi-episodic stories (such as *sean-sgéalta*, *finnscéalta*, and *scéalta gaisce*). Tom lives and works out from Miltown Malbay, in west Clare. All but one of the Clare storytellers (Jacko McGann) knew Mr. Munnelly and had at least a few of their stories recorded by him. As the example of Francie Kennelly indicates, it is Mr. Munnelly's collecting activities in the area which function to bring the individuals with knowledge of the storytelling tradition and sufficient courage to the fore; it is rarely their reputations as storytellers. Not only has the popularity of traditional storytelling declined in the competition with more modern forms of entertainment during the course of this century, particularly radio and television, but the narrators of the long, multi-episodic stories no longer have an *informed* audience for whom to perform. Narrators such as Francie Kennelly and Junior Crehan may occasionally have the opportunity to tell these stories in physical settings that approximate the traditional contexts of the past (around the fireplace or in casual social gatherings), but they are rarely, if ever, narrating for individuals who are equally knowledgeable about the tradition and capable of fully appreciating or aesthetically evaluating the performance. Thus it is the *collector*, in this case Mr. Munnelly, for whom those around Miltown who have been storytellers, or who now consider themselves such, perform, and by whom this performance is evaluated. The reality of a statement Mr. Kennelly made that in his father's time "there was no such thing...as being well known as a storyteller" lies in the fact that at the time there must have been no resident collector in the area to bring the local tradition bearers into prominence. Bairbre Ó Floinn functions in the same capacity for those tradition bearers with whom she works.

I believe that this state of affairs reveals the essential difference between the implications of the activities of the collectors of "the early days" and those of the present. When Ó Duilearga comments that Stiofán Ó hEalaoire "was much sought after as a storyteller" after many of his tales had been recorded, we know he meant "by those who were also storytellers, or enjoyed stories, or were interested in the narrative tradition in the locality," however few they may have been. Today, when the passive bearers of tradition—Francie Kennelly, Frank Anderson, and others—are somehow brought out as "traditional storytellers," there is really no concrete tradition, as there was in the past, to which they can return and contribute. If this is the case, to what tradition do the individuals involved actually belong? To answer this question the entire process must be assessed in a larger frame of reference, one in which self-consciousness, on a collective level, plays a significant part.

County Clare: A Symbiosis of Music and Storytelling

To examine the problem of self-consciousness in the storytelling tradition, I return to the subject of Co. Clare, which I will examine as a particular "culture area," one that can be seen as a microcosm of Ireland as a whole. Although Clare is very beautiful, it is somewhat out of the way, and it is not likely to appear at the top of the average tourist's list of "places to go" in Ireland. Among Irish people, however, Clare is one of the counties most associated with traditional life and ways, and it is popular with those seeking some contact with Irish rural life. Because it is less a tourist spot than other areas of the country, its economy is geared less completely to outsiders; one senses that it has a life of its own. This seems particularly true of Miltown Malbay, which is a good-sized town by Irish standards. (In contrast, social life in some country towns and rural areas seems to collapse when the tourist season ends.) One also perceives in Clare a continuity in the traditional artistic forms of the area, particularly the musical tradition; it is one of the major areas of the country, outside Dublin, for the performance of traditional music.[13] Aficionados of Irish traditional music come to Clare, especially to Miltown, Doolin, Quilty, and Ennistymon, from all parts of the world to participate in, or to listen to, the sessions of traditional music that are conducted there at all times of the year. Young people interested in learning and playing traditional tunes and styles come down from Dublin on the weekends to participate in these sessions. Because of the tremendous resurgence of this music which began in the 1960s, musicians who were known only locally twenty years ago have risen to national and even international prominence as exponents of this tradition. But it is impossible for the participants in a tradition that has received this amount of outside attention to remain completely unaffected by it, or for the tradition itself to remained unchanged.

One can sense in these areas that the musical tradition, as one finds it expressed on the local level, no longer exists solely for the inhabitants of a vicinity—its participants or those who simply enjoy it; it has a wider frame of reference. Its popularity is also fed from the outside—outside individual localities and outside the country—by the demand for Irish music originally generated in the 1960s by "The Chieftains" and, later, by other traditional groups that also achieved international recognition (such as "Planxty," "The Bothy Band," and "Clannad"). Irish traditional music is now popular and available all over the world. Some participants in the tradition—musicians and singers—have received considerable attention from companies that produce recordings of traditional music, and some are part of commercial ventures (including ones involving recordings and cassettes) of which they would probably never have dreamed twenty years ago.[14]

Irish traditional music has a very different ethos to that of most forms of popular music. Local musicians of this type are rarely "entertainers" as we understand this word, and performer-audience repartee is often minimal to nonexistent. Although individual excellence is certainly recognized, in most contemporary performances, traditional musicians are ensemble players, however informal the basis of the group; it is not part of this tradition to push oneself forward as a "star." In the many pubs all over the country in which I attended sessions of traditional music, the musicians usually sat around in a circle. Little commentary was directed to the audience, and the members of the audience usually felt few or no compunctions about making noise or carrying on conversations during the performance. Occasionally, when someone wished to sing, the proprietor might try to quiet the group. In localities regarded as centers for traditional music, such those I have noted in Co. Clare, the musicians and singers are much more likely to be the center of attention.

Because of the sudden popularity of Irish music on this unprecedented scale, many previously local musicians have received unanticipated attention and acclaim. They are suddenly "producers" of a "commodity" for which there is great demand. This requires a certain personal transition on the part of the musicians involved. The musicians are no longer performing just for themselves, but are aware of the eyes of the world upon them and of the fact that "Irishness" itself—all of the romantic images and the sense of history that Ireland, having had its own diaspora, evokes for many people—has a great deal to do with the popularity of this music. In this sense, then, the tradition is more self-conscious: the musicians are in the spotlight as never before, and they are aware of representing something more than themselves.

Although my concern here is not primarily with the musical tradition, the relationship between traditional life and traditional music in Clare is, to some degree, a symbiotic one. The interest in traditional music tends to increase the interest in, and awareness of, other traditional expressive forms, including storytelling. For example, at the time that I was leaving Ireland in April of 1984, storytelling in English, in the traditional style, was being planned as part of the agenda for the upcoming Willie Clancy Summer School, a major festival of traditional music held annually in Miltown, which attracts many people of all ages (but particularly the young) who are interested in music of this kind. The organizers intended to invite narrators whom they felt the audience would be able to understand and to follow. (John Campbell, Junior Crehan, and Donal Moore were prospective participants.) In formulating these plans, they were implicitly recognizing that this is a storytelling tradition to which very few contemporary Irish people have had any exposure whatsoever, regardless of where they live.

In scheduling traditional storytelling as part of the summer school, the organizers probably had several ideas in mind. First of all, I believe they wanted to provide the festival participants with one of the few opportunities they would probably ever have to listen to the narrating of traditional storytellers. Second, they wished to give the narrators of stories in English a forum in which to narrate for a relatively large audience, one that would presumably be interested and receptive. Third, they knew these activities would also serve to affirm the area's identity as a part of Ireland where traditional life and creative forms are still valued and performed. The Irish musical tradition has always been a vital one, and there has been no disruption in its development. It has survived the rapid social changes of this century and is even thriving. Why not utilize such a context in the attempt to revitalize, or at least to maintain some continuity in, a tradition that has long been struggling for its existence?

In light of the above comments, we can return to the question of the tradition to which such storytellers belong. The situation in Clare reflects the changes Irish life has undergone generally. We can see in the developments there an attempt to give such storytellers something approximating a natural role in the artistic life of the community. It is a compromise of sorts. The frame of reference that the narrators and the audience share is some sense of the value of the old, traditional ways and the aesthetic accomplishments of generations of Irish country people, something that is part of their collective heritage and experience. But the storytellers are now performing for an audience whose members are almost completely unfamiliar with the narrative tradition, who cannot critically appreciate or evaluate their performances and, more than likely, will never be able to do so. Unlike the musical performances at the festival, there is nothing artistically at stake here. The majority of the narrators, to some degree, have adopted this role and are narrating in such settings because it is the *role* itself that is valued; they are not necessarily valued for the excellence of their storytelling. There is manifest self-consciousness here. It is the infatuation with the past and the lack of clear standards by which to judge critically the narrative performances of the storytellers which make it possible for certain individuals in such a position to take up the mantle of "traditional storyteller" with relative ease. This, in essence, sums up the state, and the problems, of the narrative tradition in English as a whole.

Some of the storytellers living in other parts of the country who have been given opportunities to narrate in relatively public settings are disenfranchised from the roots of the tradition to a greater degree than those "protected" by the ambience of Co. Clare. Frank Anderson and Elizabeth Bourke, for example, both appeared on a television program and told stories about unusual local happenings, as I mentioned. Although I did not see the program, I have listened to many Irish radio programs in which some of the "old people" of a locality were interviewed about such matters. However kindly they are treated, one frequently senses that they are being exhibited as relics of the unsophisticated, rural past to the general, and more urbane, public. At times the inherent condescension is but thinly concealed.[15] Similarly, when Mr. Anderson or Mrs. Bourke, or someone like them, has the opportunity to narrate in such settings, they are not really serving as representatives of a narrative tradition or performing for an audience of peers. They are functioning symbolically as mediators between Ireland's predominantly rural past and its increasingly urban present.[16] The audience and the narrators represent markedly different spheres of contemporary Irish life, between which there is now a considerable gap. To whatever degree such programs provide information about Irish cultural history, they provide very little concrete information to modern audiences about the storytelling tradition. For these reasons aesthetic judgments of any kind on the part of the audience *relative to the storytelling tradition of the past* (such as judgments regarding the narrators' knowledge or use of traditional motifs and themes, ability to construct and resolve complex plots, or mastery of the customary language of traditional storytelling) are null considerations. The role of "storyteller" in such contexts is one for which the requirements can be met by almost anyone who is able and willing to relate accounts of unusual happenings in settings of this kind.

THE INFLUENCE OF EAMON KELLY

The effects of Eamon Kelly's storytelling upon the Irish public are pertinent to the present discussion. Mr. Kelly is, as noted in the Introduction, Ireland's foremost commercially successful storyteller. He has been performing through various media—television, radio, books, recordings, the stage—for decades. By adopting the persona of "The Shanachie," he has consciously used and exploited the comic potential of the image of the Irish countryman, a long-standing and stock figure of Anglo-Irish tradition.[17] Kelly is a native Kerryman (from Glenflesk) and a fluent speaker of Irish; he is also familiar with, and has been a participant in, storytelling sessions in the areas of west Cork and Kerry.

When Kelly began telling stories on the radio in the 1950s, he was in need of new material for his broadcasts. Several sources presented themselves: his fan mail contained many traditional stories that people took the trouble to write down and send to him. When he had occasion to return to the west, particularly Cork and Kerry, people knew who he was, and they would arrange storytelling sessions for him to attend. In addition, Kelly made the acquaintance of several narrators of the long, traditional tales who lived in the vicinity of Glenflesk; he also acquired some of his stories from published collections of folktales.

Mr. Kelly had experienced the storytelling tradition in both Irish and English, and he modeled his original narrating style on the first traditional storyteller he had heard. Traditional narrating tends to be relatively straightforward and, although there are regional variations in this, not typically very "dramatic" in the modern sense of that term. Over the years Kelly has modified his early storytelling style to suit his current medium of performance. (Storytelling to a theatre audience, for instance, requires a dramatic performance of a different nature than narrating in the intimate context of fireside chat.) The style he now employs, as I have heard it on the radio and records, is much more dramatic than is usual among the traditional storytellers with whom I am familiar. He varies both the amplification and the inflections in his voice greatly. He uses his knowledge of rural customs and folkways to set the stage for his tales, most of which are short, humorous vignettes about country life and people. Although some of these are jokes with punch lines or stories involving clever retorts, much of the humor in his narration is derived from the "vocal" characteristics of his storytelling: the ironic, arch, and slightly self-mocking tone of his delivery. As John Campbell says of Eamon Kelly's narrating, "It's his flow of speech...the way he tells them—he holds you."

Mr. Kelly's storytelling falls in the breach between the reality of the old storytelling tradition and the general public's awareness of that tradition. The Irish population was predominantly rural until relatively recently; rural depopulation has occurred in Ireland on a tremendous scale relative to the period of time involved.[18] By consciously using the image of the rural storyteller, "the shanachie," and by incorporating realistic details of country life into his narrating, Kelly has reacquainted many Irish people—particularly young city dwellers—with both a way of life and a tradition of which they had but dim, if any, awareness. (For some, of course, it was a life only recently left behind.) He has become, to a certain extent, a national symbol for the storytelling tradition of the past.[19]

Because Mr. Kelly's performances are the only exposure many Irish people have had to the tradition, a secondary effect of these productions has been the creation of an auxiliary model for storytelling in English which exerts its own pull on the populace and on the activity of storytelling in general: all over Ireland one encounters people telling Eamon's stories and sounding very much like him while doing so. This is true even of some individuals who have been exposed to, or have participated in, more traditional storytelling, including some of the narrators discussed herein. Peter Kelleher is a friend and avid fan of Eamon's and enjoys learning and telling his stories. Seán Ó Duinnín, a narrator of stories in Irish, considers Mr. Kelly "a good English storyteller." John Campbell describes him as "the greatest [storyteller] I ever listened to."

The results of all this are somewhat mixed in terms of the public's perception of traditional storytelling. Mr. Kelly's activities as a professional entertainer have increased the public's awareness of the storytelling tradition and of the role of the storyteller while concurrently modifying the public's conception of them in subtle but significant ways.[20] Important distinctions between *scéalaí* and *seanchaí* in terms of narrative repertoire and social function have been melded in his characterization of the rural storyteller, and he has presented a quite untypical style of narrating in association with traditional storytelling. The public's notions about the tradition have been molded by Kelly's portrayals of the shanachie, resulting in a broader conception of the "Irish" storyteller and storytelling, one that has little to do with the demands of the roles of *seanchaí* or *scéalaí* and is much more marketable; furthermore, it is one that makes it considerably easier for contemporary Irish people to fulfill the expectations of this kind of performance. As I perceive it, the direction in which Mr. Kelly's narrative style has pulled modern ideas about the tradition has now become *the* direction in which any popular, contemporary storytelling that attempts to communicate the characteristics of Irish rural life or people is going to go. The demand for Kelly's stories and the way he tells them make him the outstanding model, in terms of style and repertoire, for those storytellers who wish to appeal to a very general audience, such as John Campbell and Peter Kelleher, both of whom perform in relatively large social gatherings. Because the expectations of modern audiences have been conditioned by the material to which they have been exposed, further departure from the telling of the long, structurally complex, and often less obviously humorous tales (*sean-sgéalta, finnscéalta,* and *scéalta gaisce* [hero tales]) seems inevitable.

In the above discussion, I have hinted at problem areas without discussing them in depth: the heretofore important distinctions between the *scéalaí* and *seanchaí* in the storytelling tradition and the highly problematic subject of the bases for aesthetic judgments of Irish storytelling in the English language. Because both problems are related to the differential treatment of the participants in the two language traditions, I will defer discussion of this and related topics—assumptions about the differences between the two language traditions and the preponderance of collecting activity in *Gaeltacht* areas—for Chapter Three of this study.

LIMITATIONS IN THE DOCUMENTATION OF THE TRADITION

The last topic I wish to discuss within the framework of the influence of collectors and collecting activities in the tradition is the subject of the role of women in Irish storytelling. I wish to present this topic as representative of a very particular ethnographic problem. The results of my research in Ireland support the generalizations about the role of women in the storytelling tradition that I presented in the Introduction: first, that women participated less than men; second, that men rather than women tended to be the narrators of the longer, multi-episodic tales, such as *Märchen* and hero tales (*sean-sgéalta* and *scéalta gaisce,* respectively); third, that it was also considered inappropriate for women to tell hero tales, particularly those of the Fenian cycle (*finnscéalta*); and fourth, as a corollary to these points, that men and women usually went visiting separately. There were notable exceptions to the supposed inferiority of women as narrators of the long stories (such as famed woman narrator, Peig Sayers), but there is a general lack of information about women storytellers, the types of stories women told, and the contexts in which they participated in the tradition.[21] The lacunae in the record concerning the role of women are but a reflection of the lack of documentation for the tradition as a whole; moreover, limitations imposed by the lack of women folklore collectors and by culturally defined roles for both sexes may have very particular implications in terms of our knowledge of the role of women in the tradition.

As I have observed, the Irish government's attempt at a systematic documentation of what was considered to be a "dying tradition" began in the first half of this century. The early collectors recorded the traditions of Irish country people, including the stories that they told, in writing; later they used the Ediphone machine. In the interest of governmental economy, the material recorded on the Ediphone's wax cylinders was transcribed by the collectors and then erased so that the cylinders could be reused. The result was the destruction of many original voice recordings. The Ediphone was ultimately displaced by more sophisticated and economical recording equipment (such as tape recorders), making more durable records possible. However, no increase in sophistication of equipment can change the fact that, technologically, no complete record—visual and aural—of any storytelling situation was possible until very recently, a time when the natural, informal contexts for storytelling among informed participants had almost ceased to exist.[22]

In addition to the technological limitations inherent in the early documentation, which hindsight allows the luxury of appraising, it was limited in other respects as well. The various governmental agencies involved in collecting in Ireland have always been pressed for funds and resources (hence the recycling of the Ediphone cylinders). In spite of the highest ideals and aspirations, it has never been possible for the fieldworkers to cover the entire country in anything approaching systematic and comprehensive depth, a situation I believe Irish folklore scholars would be the first to acknowledge. There has always been a shortage of collectors relative to the demands of the task at hand.

The lack of resources pertains to the lack of information concerning the role of women in two ways. Generally, it has simply never been possible to document *all* the aspects of the tradition or all the social situations of which storytelling was a part. In fact, there is woefully little in situ documentation of Irish storytelling at all.[23] More specifically, and potentially far more important, I have encountered almost no references to women collectors. Setting aside Lady Augusta Gregory's unique contribution to Irish folklore and literature, since the early days of folklore collecting the overwhelming majority of the collectors have been men. This has important implications in terms of what we know about women's storytelling. Although it was not invariably the case, it was generally customary for men and women to go *ar cuairt* separately; and we really have no exact information as to what kinds of stories women told in the gatherings in which *only* women participated except to assume that they continued to follow to some degree the traditional norms of appropriateness for storytelling. In addition to the groups involved in nightly visiting, there may have been other such all-female groups. For example, the collector Seán Ó hEochaidh described to me a form of transhumance practiced in Donegal until about one hundred years ago. During the summer, groups of women would take their cattle from the lowlands up to the mountains where they lived in small cabins (*bothóga*) built for this purpose.[24] Seán said that he knew they had *ceilis* and sang songs, but there is no record of whether or not they told stories. It seems extremely probable to me, given such isolated social conditions, that they would have. Even if a collector had been present in either of these two kinds of settings, the presence of a *male* collector in such groups would unquestionably alter the dynamics of group interaction and the nature of the stories being told. What I wish to suggest here is highly speculative, but it is *possible* that women in such contexts did not find it necessary to conform completely to the societal norms for behavior in "mixed" groups, as they do not in our own culture; that more women may have narrated than did so in mixed company; and that more may have ventured to tell the kinds of stories usually associated with men: hero tales, *Märchen*, and, possibly, even off-color or obscene material. We simply have no in situ documentation of storytelling in such settings upon which to judge. This situation represents an intriguing ethnographic problem, but one which, at this time, is undoubtedly beyond amelioration.[25]

I have attempted in this chapter to illustrate the importance of the role of Irish folklore collectors in the preservation and perpetuation of the tradition, and to indicate that folklore collecting in Ireland is itself a "tradition" with its own continuities with the past. At this point in time, the activities of collectors cannot be conceived of as subsidiary to the tradition, at least not the tradition of telling the long, structurally complex tales. The collectors are often the *raison d'être* for the performance of such narratives, and frequently of other kinds of stories as well. The narrators discussed in this overview represent the most clearly discernible trends in terms of the effects that contact with collectors has had on individuals in their capacity as storytellers, and the implications such contact has for them personally and for the tradition. The collectors "keep it all going" and provide various social incentives—formally and informally—for people to tell "the old stories." It is not at all surprising, considering their importance at the local level, that traditional storytelling seems to disappear completely in some areas that have no active collectors, or that Máire Nic Aodha would comment on the decline of the tradition in Na Cruacha, Co. Donegal, where she lives, in terms of collector Seán Ó hEochaidh's retirement: "the old stories went with Seán."

Notes to Chapter Two

1. Caoimhín Ó Danachair, "The Irish Folklore Commission," *The Folklore and Folk Music Archivist* 1 (Spring 1961): 4.

2. According to Carl Wilhelm von Sydow, "passive bearers" of tradition (of any kind) are those who are familiar with it but are not active in its transmission. "Active bearers" (also, "traditors") are involved in the tradition and in its dissemination. In the case of folktales, they are performers of narratives. See C. W. von Sydow, "Geography and Folk-Tale Oicotypes," in *Selected Papers on Folklore*, ed. Laurits Bødker (Copenhagen: Rosenkilde & Bagger, 1948; reprint ed., New York: Arno Press, 1977), p.49.

3. J. H. Delargy, "The Gaelic Story-Teller. With Some Notes on Gaelic Folk-Tales," *Proceedings of the British Academy* 31 (1945): 188.

4. Ibid., p. 189. Delargy does not indicate here how or why Ó hEalaoire came to his attention, but J. E. Caerwyn Williams points out in his discussion of Irish storytelling that Ó hEalaoire was "a superior Gaelic speaker and conversant," which may have led Delargy to him. J. E. Caerwyn Williams, *Y Storïwr Gwyddeleg a'i Chwedlau* (Cardiff: University of Wales Press, 1972), p. 93. A collection of Ó hEalaoire's stories was published in 1981. The notes are in English, but all the texts are in Irish (with no translations). See *Leabhar Stiofáin Uí Ealaoire*, ed. Séamus Ó Duilearga (Baile Átha Cliath: Comhairle Bhéaloideas Éireann, 1981).

5. Delargy, "The Gaelic Story-Teller," pp. 197-98.

6. I was recently informed that Mr. Murrihy died in June 1990.

7. Since my conversations with Francie, professional storyteller Sharon Kennedy (from Massachusetts) has also recorded some stories from him.

8. Mr. O'Farrell's playing has been recorded for airing on *Radio Éireann* twice. I do not know if these were ensemble or solo performances.

9. This story is "The Wild Boy," a version of international Type 726 (*The Dream Visit*).

10. Mrs. Droney died in late 1984 or early 1985.

11. Although John is also an accordion player, I do not believe he was playing on this occasion.

12. I had great difficulty in getting John to talk to me at all, and I did not feel that the subject of his shyness was one I could broach—however subtly—in conversation with him.

13. County Clare also hosts the Merriman Summer School, an annual event established in 1969 and dedicated to the Gaelic literary and cultural tradition.

14. I am not suggesting that traditional musicians, as a group, hope to "get rich quick," but merely that I am sure most of them never expected to find their music on records or any commercial medium. Some of Junior Crehan's tunes, for example, were recorded by Séamas MacMathúna and can be heard on an album entitled "West Clare Fiddlers." I have also seen albums of other members of the Crehan family.

15. *Radio na Gaeltachta* has an entirely different approach and tone. It actively promotes traditions involving the Irish language for an Irish speaking audience—those who share the same frame of reference and whose own interests are furthered by these activities. For many Irish speakers, it is "their" radio station.

16. According to Ralph Linton, nativistic movements (i.e., movements that attempt to revive or perpetuate certain aspects of a culture) characteristically involve the attributing of symbolic value to particular past or present (or both) cultural elements. Linton states, "The more distinctive such elements are with respect to other cultures with which the society is in contact, the greater their potential value as symbols of the society's unique character." Ralph Linton, "Nativistic Movements," *American Anthropologist* 45 (1943): 231.

17. The figure of the Irish countryman as a coy and cunning buffoon made its first appearance in Anglo-Irish literature in the character of Thady Quirk in *Castle Rackrent*. Maria Edgeworth, *Castle Rackrent* (London: Joseph Johnson, 1800).

18. According to Ruth Dudley Edwards, "in Ireland the population of the towns in 130 years has risen only slightly while there has been massive rural depopulation." Ruth Dudley Edwards, *An Atlas of Irish History* (London: Methuen & Co., 1973: reprint ed., London and New York: Methuen & Co., 1981) p. 232.

19. I do not mean to imply that Eamon Kelly was the first or the only person to use the term *seanchaí* (English spellings, shanachie, seanachie, and others) in the English vernacular. I do feel, however, that his appropriation of this term, and its subsequent presentation in so many commercial media, are the most important factors in its *current* popularity. As I noted in the Introduction, the use of this term by English speakers can be traced back at least as far as the sixteenth century. It was used frequently by Anglo-Irish writers of the nineteenth century. For example, William Carleton notes, in the "General Introduction" to *Traits and Stories of the Irish Peasantry*, that "the Senachie, where he exists, is but a dim and faded representative of that very old Chronicler in his palmy days...." William Carleton, *Traits and Stories of the Irish Peasantry*, 5th ed., 2 vols. (London: George Routledge & Co., 1856), p. xxiii. A short-lived periodical, *The Shanachie: An Irish Miscellany*, was published in Dublin from 1906 to 1907. Vivian Mercier informed me (personal conversation, March 29, 1987) that the Irish author Seumas MacManus, a native Irish speaker from Donegal, played this role (i.e., that of "shanachie") on the stage in New York sometime during the first half of this century.

20. Mr. Kelly told me that it has never been his intention to be absolutely true to the storytelling tradition or to portray it accurately to the public. He is aware of it and uses material from it as a resource in his dramatic presentations (personal conversation with Mr. Kelly, April 2, 1984).

21. Delargy presents these generalizations in "The Gaelic Story-Teller," p. 181.

22. I am aware that video recordings of traditional storytellers and musicians are now being made at the Department of Irish Folklore at University College, Dublin, at Trinity College (Dublin), and at University College, Galway. They are probably made at other institutions as well.

23. Lack of contextual information—about the storytellers and the situations for storytelling—is characteristic of most of the early collections of folktales. A notable exception is Jeremiah Curtin's *Tales of the Fairies and of the Ghost World Collected from Oral Tradition in South-West Munster* (London: Alfred Nutt, 1895), in which some information is provided about the individual storytellers from whom, and the on-going contexts in which, Curtin heard the stories. Henry Glassie, *Passing the Time in Ballymenone: Culture and History of an Ulster Community* (Philadelphia: University of Pennsylvania Press, 1982), is an in-depth study of the traditions of an Ulster community and includes a great deal of material on historical narratives, their narrators, and the contexts of narration. Historical texts have been extracted from this voluminous study and can be found in Henry Glassie, *Irish Folk History* (Philadelphia: University of Pennsylvania Press, 1982).

24. The 1943 issue of *Béaloideas* (volume 13) contains three articles (one of which is in English) on Irish forms of transhumance. See Seán Ó hEochaidh, "Buailteachas í dTír Chonaill," pp. 130-58; Seán Ó Cathasaigh, "Buailíochaí in iarthar Chonamara," pp. 159-60; and Pádraig Ó Moghráin, "Some Mayo Traditions of the *Buaile*," pp. 161-71.

25. For further consideration of these and other aspects of the problem of evaluating the role of women in the Irish storytelling tradition, see Clodagh Brennan Harvey, "Some Irish Women Storytellers and Reflections on the Role of Women in the Storytelling Tradition," *Western Folklore* 48 (1989): 109-28.

3

THE CURRENT STATUS OF THE TWO LANGUAGE TRADITIONS

DEVELOPMENTS IN THE STUDY OF TRADITIONAL NARRATIVE

As we have seen, by the beginning of the twentieth century the interest in Irish folklore had become firmly linked to the Literary Revival and to the cause of Irish nationalism. The emphasis of the early folklore collectors on Gaelic language materials grew out of a profound sense of cultural loss—a loss epitomized by the loss of the Irish language—and the need for the affirmation of cultural identity stressed by the newly formed national government in the late 1920s. Developments at the political and social level are reflected in the evolution of Irish folklore studies, particularly in the area of traditional narrative.

The division between the literary and the scholarly treatment of Irish traditional narrative material actually became complete through and after the work of Douglas Hyde, whose influence is deeply imprinted on Irish folklore studies.[1] Hyde became the first president of Ireland in 1938, but his career had begun in serious linguistic study. With Eoin MacNeill, Hyde founded the Gaelic League (1893), a society dedicated to the goal of revivifying and representing to the Irish people, through various literary forms, the old Gaelic culture and language. Between 1889 and 1939 Hyde wrote a number of works on various aspects of Irish literature and tradition, several volumes of which included texts of folktales. Among the most influential of these was *Beside the Fire*, published in 1890.[2] This event marks the turning point for the treatment of traditional narratives by Irish folklore scholars and collectors.

Beside the Fire is a collection of fourteen Irish-Gaelic narratives (six with translations into English) of which Hyde was the collector, translator, and commentator. Hyde takes on a number of issues of importance to folklorists, such as the role of the individual narrator in the tradition and the problems involved in collecting and translating story texts. Because Hyde was explicitly involved in the preservation of what he considered to be a dying tradition, his central concern was the issue of fidelity to the spoken Irish; Hyde called for a thorough knowledge of the Irish language on the part of anyone working with Irish folklore and narrative.

It is on these grounds in *Beside the Fire* that Hyde evaluates the work of his major predecessors, including T. Crofton Croker, Patrick Kennedy, Lady Wilde, and the Irish-American collector, Jeremiah Curtin, all of whom had published collections of oral tales. The attempts of the Irish collectors at presenting Irish traditional tales are, from Hyde's standpoint, "interesting from a literary point of view...[but] not always successes from a scientific one," for none of them was fluent in the language, and they freely embellished and reworked their narrative materials for popular audiences.[3] Furthermore, they also provided very little or no background information about the sources of their narratives. Although Hyde acknowledges that Jeremiah Curtin "approached the fountainhead more nearly than any other,"[4] for Curtin was the first to record his tales directly from Gaelic speakers (through the medium of an interpreter) and tampered less with the original material, Hyde also takes Curtin to task for his lack of knowledge of the language: "...his ignorance of the commonest Irish words is as startling as Lady Wilde's."[5] Hyde regarded the record of the oral storytelling tradition as preserved in English language narratives, which up to this time constituted the bulk of the documentation of Irish oral folktales, as a markedly inferior record of the glories of Gaelic narrative and storytelling. According to Hyde,

> ...when the skeletons were thus padded round and clad, although built upon folk-lore, they were no longer folk-lore themselves, for folk-lore can only find a fitting garment in the language that comes from the mouths of those whose minds are so primitive that they retain with pleasure those tales which the more sophisticated invariably forget. For this reason, folk-lore is presented in an uncertain and unsuitable medium, whenever the contents of the stories are divorced from their original expression in language.[6]

Deeply influenced by the work of Hyde on folktales and other native genres, folklorists and writers of the Literary Revival (Lady Gregory, Yeats, Synge, and others), dedicated themselves to the task of documenting faithfully the spoken word in both languages, Irish and English.

AESTHETIC CONSIDERATIONS IN TRADITIONAL STORYTELLING
The Preeminence of the Irish Language Tradition

When the systematic documentation of Irish traditional culture began in the early decades of this century, the intention of the early folklore collectors was to preserve a legacy of the achievements of the old, Gaelic Ireland. This preoccupation is understandable historically given the devastating repercussions of British activities in Ireland. However, the underlying assumption that the tradition of oral storytelling in English is merely an inferior offshoot of that in Irish has been remarkably tenacious over the ensuing decades despite the fact that some parts of Ireland have been dominated by Britain, and have been English in custom and language, for many centuries. (As early as 1366 the Irish parliament, under pressure from the English crown, legally established an English-speaking area of Ireland, referred to as "the Pale," which included Dublin and a substantial part of the eastern seaboard of Ireland as well.[7]) Because so much of the early collecting activity focused on storytellers and their tales,[8] the persistence of the notion of the inferiority of the English language tradition has also resulted in several paradoxical developments for the storytelling traditions in both languages as they coexist today. In tracing these developments I will begin with a discussion of the assumed similarities and differences in the two traditions, proceed to the findings of my own research, and then examine their implications for the tradition of Irish oral storytelling as a whole.

The two major branches of traditional storytelling are, as I have noted, *seanchas* and *scéalaíocht*, and the narrators of tales in the two categories, *seanchaí* and *scéalaí*, respectively; Irish storytellers have tended to specialize in one or the other of these branches of the tradition. (There are also many subcategories of the two branches.) Although the focus of scholarly attention has been on the traditions of the *Gaeltacht* areas, the documentation of the tradition has nevertheless always involved the recording of traditional materials, including narratives, in the English-speaking parts of the country as well.[9] The nomenclature described here, which was derived from Gaelic language materials, is applied to the narrators and stories of the tradition in English. Traditional storytellers in English tell the same kinds of stories as storytellers in Irish.[10] They employ similar structuring principles and draw from a collective pool of content elements (including dramatis personae, motifs, and sequences of episodes).

Most scholarship that deals with the differences in the tales in the two language traditions finds the English language narratives inferior to those in Irish primarily on the bases of the quality and the kind of language employed or the degree of structural development; these points are reiterated consistently throughout the commentary on the English language tradition. For example, in "The Gaelic Story-Teller" Delargy states in regard to Irish *Märchen* narrated in English that "although many folk-tales of this kind have been recorded in English, the Anglo-Irish wonder-tale...compares very unfavorably both as to style and content with similar tales in Irish."[11] In *Beside the Fire*, Douglas Hyde goes even further to assert regarding Gaelic myths in the English language that "English-speaking people either do not know them at all, or else tell them in so bald and condensed a form as to be useless."[12]

The language of the two narrative traditions is unquestionably different. Although there is some use of formulaic diction in English-language narratives, the language of these tales is easily comprehended and more closely approaches that of everyday speech. For the narrator of *scéalaíocht* in Irish it was not enough to be a good Irish speaker and rhetorician; to be considered a master of his art he was expected to avoid trite and prosaic words and phrases and to express himself in original and striking ways.[13] The aesthetic canons of the tradition required him to exhibit virtuosic control of a special category of language associated with Irish storytelling, called *crua-Ghaedhilg* or *crua-Ghaolainn*, literally, "hard Irish." This was Irish quite unlike that of everyday speech; it was more grammatical and had an archaic quality.[14] Furthermore, narrators of such stories, particularly the hero tales (*scéalta gaisce*), were expected to incorporate into their narrating passages of obscure, archaic prose, called "runs," parts of which are incomprehensible even to Irish speakers. (These "runs" have various names in Irish, depending on what they describe [for example, *cóiriú catha*, "preparation for battle," or *cóiriú farraige*, "preparation for a voyage"] and are somewhat similar to the formulaic descriptions found in the Homeric epics.[15])

Aesthetic judgments of Irish Gaelic storytelling were based on the display of linguistic virtuosity. In his work on the Irish storytelling tradition, *Y Storïwr Gwyddeleg a'i Chwedlau* (*The Irish Storyteller and His Tales*), J. E. Caerwyn Williams relates several anecdotes about individuals noted for their command of this "hard

Irish." Séamas Ó hAirt was Douglas Hyde's first informant and the only narrator Hyde met who could tell a story in "hard Irish." One Mici Seanlaigh bet Ó hAirt a gallon of *poitín* (illicit whiskey) that he could translate any of Ó hAirt's stories into English. A houseful of people gathered for this event, and when Ó hAirt began to tell a story about Finn and the fianna in the "hard Irish," Seanlaigh was utterly unable to render it into English. Seán Chormaic Í Shé, a *seanchaí* and *scéalaí*, was interested in unusual words and expressions and was proud of his mastery of the *crua-Ghaedhilg*. Ó Duilearga visited Seán not long before the latter died, and the only thing troubling the sick man at this time was the meaning of certain things in *crua-Ghaedhilg*.[16] Linguistic excellence and dexterity *for its own sake* was the most important yardstick by which the narrator of stories in Irish was measured.[17]

When I began my research in Ireland, I was more concerned with the social factors influencing the storytelling tradition than I was with problems of aesthetics. After listening to several narrators of stories in English (Packie Murrihy, Junior Crehan, Martin McKenna, Katie Droney, and others) recount many long, complicated tales, I began to ponder the question of what it was they strove for in their narrating. Based on the stories only, it was a question I found very difficult to answer. After talking to a number of narrators of stories in Irish, which I did in the later phase of my research, I became aware that a vacuum seemed to exist in the English language tradition in regard to the aesthetic criteria for such storytelling. The few times that I broached this subject with those who narrate in English—what was important in the story, or what effect the narrator was trying to bring about—I encountered a real void. They did not seem to be cognizant of any goals for which they were striving; they were simply "telling the stories." John Campbell is a case in point. When I queried him about his own storytelling, what he tried to accomplish, he replied, "I don't know why I tell them. I really don't know. I just tell them." The only concrete answer that I received from narrators in English to my probings on this subject was "wanting to be funny." But this response—from Peter Kelleher and John Campbell—was in reference to the telling of jokes and amusing anecdotes in public settings, not to the telling of structurally complex tales. Feeling I had reached a dead end on this topic, I stopped pursuing it until some time later when my conversations with narrators in Irish again drew my attention to it.

In discussing such concerns with several Irish language storytellers, I found that it was not a question with which they had to struggle. Their responses were immediate and clearly articulated: their primary concern was with the language itself, not plot development, or characterization, or any other possibilities. As Seán Ó Duinnín put it, "I try to give out as much of the fluent Irish that's in the story. I tell it for the sake of the vocabulary." Donal Moore, who narrates in both languages, has a decided preference for narrating in Irish because of the greater intellectual challenge it poses for him. Donal acknowledges, "I don't get the same kick in 'em [stories in English] that would be in Irish...There's more talent in it." For the native Irish narrators used to the formulaic and archaic diction of the storytelling tradition, the challenge in telling such stories lies in the opportunity they provide for them to exhibit their command of the special language of the storytelling tradition.[18]

It is my contention that the lack of a clearly defined *native* aesthetic canon or set of criteria for assessing storytelling in English may have played a vital part in the differential treatment afforded the narrators in the two traditions. Disregarding for the moment the nationalistic thrust of Irish folklore collecting, one can note that it is certainly the personal prerogative of scholars in any discipline to pursue those areas that they find intellectually more stimulating, as Irish scholars manifestly have found the Irish language tradition to be. In addition, because there is some consensus among scholars and storytellers regarding the current aesthetic criteria for storytelling in Irish, the tradition in Irish is one that is more easily amenable to critical evaluation, a factor that also must have a certain appeal to scholars. There appears to be no such consensus regarding the tradition in English.

Just how far back in time the present vagueness of the thinking about aesthetic factors on the part of the narrators in English extends is difficult to ascertain. Certainly, the tradition of storytelling of this kind (or any tradition, for that matter) would not have persisted as long as it has if there were no reasons for either telling or listening to these tales. I believe that this is a comparatively recent development and that it is linked to the virtual disappearance, for narrators in English, of an informed audience for their storytelling. The solitary evidence I have for this assertion is my recording session with Jack Mahony and John Reilly. This is the only session during the course of my research in which I had to deal with the *active* participation of more than one person at the same time. I felt that this session at least approximated the experience of storytelling and *listening* in the contexts of the past, contexts in which the members of the audience were familiar with the tradition and customary participants in it.

The significance of the presence of *both* men can be appreciated fully only when the results of the two recording sessions I had with Jack Mahony are compared. When I interviewed Jack alone, he had great difficulty remembering his stories and a certain reluctance to attempt to tell them. During the interview with John Reilly, at which Jack was present, Jack was extremely garrulous, frequently diverting the conversation to other topics and interjecting comments and stories during John's narrating; in this context, I had difficultly in getting Jack *not* to narrate.

Whether or not John or Jack could actually articulate what each expected of the other, there was constant interaction between them, regardless of who was narrating. The intensity of the interaction revealed the importance of the presence of an informed audience to the performance of the storyteller, for the comments of each seemed to provide support for the current narrator and an on-going affirmation of the accuracy and truth of the events being described. In essence, each storyteller endorsed the performances of the other. The lack of such performance contexts today relegates the narrators of traditional stories in English to a contextual void in which they function more as symbolic representatives of Ireland's rural past than as active participants in a living art form.

The situation is quite different for narrators in the native language tradition. Despite the ongoing decline in this century in the number of native Irish speakers in the *Gaeltacht* areas,[19] narrators of stories in Irish remain the primary focus of current collecting activity and of the scholarship on traditional narrative. Relative to the English-language tradition, the tradition in Irish can be said to be thriving. Narrators of the long, traditional tales in Irish do have an audience for their stories. For those storytellers who wish to participate, there is a national competition every year (the *Oireachtas*) which includes traditional storytelling (in Irish only) among its events.[20] Participants are judged on the basis of their linguistic virtuosity; they are expected to be able to narrate the long, multi-episodic tales (*scéalaíocht*) and to incorporate the rhetorical descriptive passages associated with Irish heroic narrative ("runs"). These competitions do not allow any kind of personal experience narratives, *siscéalta*, or other shorter forms (*seanchas*) because the formulaic descriptive passages are not customarily a part of such stories. Several storytellers I interviewed (Donal Moore, Seán Ó Duinnín, Seán McDermot, Éamonn Ó Donnghaile, and others) had entered or adjudicated (or both) at the *Oireachtas* on a number of occasions. Because they had heard and seen each other perform, they were aware of the degree of mastery of the tradition each had achieved. They could articulate what they felt to be the strengths and weaknesses of each other's styles, and they were aware of the regional differences represented in individual styles. (Seán Ó hEochaidh, the retired Donegal collector, noted that the more modern storytellers in Donegal are not as dramatic as the ones of the past, but "more like professors now than real storytellers." In contrast, Galway storyteller Éamonn Ó Donnghaile commented rather negatively on the unnatural, excessively "dramatic" style of the Donegal narrators he had recently seen at the *Oireachtas*. Éamonn characterized the style of Kerry, Clare, and Mayo as "quiet but impressive.")

The benefits of these competitions are not limited to the prizes the participants win or to the acclaim and attention they receive for their performances. The very existence of the competition gives the storytellers in Irish a sense that they are participants in a valued tradition, regardless of the present state of that tradition in the general population. These competitions allow them to overcome, to some degree, the decline of the tradition at the local level because they make it possible for the participants to form, however loosely knit, a national confraternity of peers. In such settings the storytellers are narrating to an informed audience, capable of appreciating and aesthetically evaluating their performance. Storytellers in English, as represented by those whom I have encountered, often do not know each other and certainly do not narrate in contexts where factors such as their storytelling style or mastery of the tradition are being critically evaluated by those who are equally knowledgeable. I am not suggesting that the *Oireachtas* is the sole forum for traditional storytelling in Irish or that narrators in English have no audience whatsoever for their stories. This is not the case.[21] However, no forum with the national prestige of the *Oireachtas* exists for the narrators of traditional stories in English; nor does the creation of one, or an increase in public awareness of the tradition, seem likely unless Irish scholars show more interest in *traditional* storytelling in English. The irony in the prevailing preeminence given by folklore scholars and those interested in Irish traditional life to the narrative tradition in Irish lies in the fact that only a small proportion of the total population of Ireland is Irish speaking, and the number of Irish speakers in *Gaeltacht* areas continues to diminish, a situation that does not seem likely to change for the better.[22]

The English Language Tradition: Narrating and Narrators of *Scéalaíocht*

The problem of the difficulty of making aesthetic judgments about traditional narratives in English is related to that of determining just who is a master of this tradition. The inability on the part of some of the narrators to articulate their own criteria of excellence does not mean that they do not, or did not, have any; it does imply that such considerations have little relevance to their current motivations for narrating, at least of *scéalaíocht*. Although the language of these tales is stylized to some degree in both traditions (repetitive elements tend to be formulated in very similar ways), the highly arcane diction of narratives in Irish has no counterpart in the English language tradition. Therefore, superiority in the exhibition and control of this language is not a criterion of mastery for storytellers in English. How, then, can mastery of the narrative tradition in English be judged?

Given that the narrators could not articulate aesthetic norms for the tradition, one can infer that certain things are nonetheless expected from the experiences of telling and listening to stories. For a narrator to enlist the audience's imagination in the world of story, he or she must be sufficiently competent at generating a plot structure that requires satisfactory resolution and at providing such resolution. The structure then becomes the vehicle for the artistic embellishment characteristic of a narrator's style. The combined effect of these two elements is then what I would call the "entertainment value" of the story. One can gain some indication of the varying degrees of competency achieved by the narrators in terms of structural development and resolution by a close examination of the transcriptions of their tales. However, the subjective experience of listening to the storytellers was also a vital element in the evaluation of their performances. In some instances the storytellers seemed to be reporting rather than performing, useful conceptual distinctions made by Dell Hymes. According to Hymes, a narrative is *performed* when it is dramatized in such a way that "the standards intrinsic to the tradition in which the performance occurs are accepted and realized," and when the performer "assumes responsibility to an audience" for the presentation of the tradition.[23] A story is *reported* when it is merely related. Although *reporting* involves the recognition that an event or action is socially or culturally meaningful, it is not full performance. In the following discussion of the storytellers and their tales, I observe Hymes' distinctions.

In regard to the narrators of longer, structurally complex tales (*scéalaíocht*), Packie Murrihy, Donal Moore, and John Campbell have the greatest facility in the generation and resolution of complicated, multi-episodic plots. However, my subjective responses to their narrating were markedly different. I would describe Packie Murrihy's storytelling as "interesting" rather than "enjoyable." Like many traditional storytellers, Packie had little interest in the psychological aspects of a story, and his development of motivation and character were both minimal. His storytelling style was undramatic even by the standards of traditional storytelling. Packie told very long and complicated tales, and seemed to focus on the evolution and denouement of a complex story line. There were several problems in his narrating, however, which made sections of his stories very difficult to follow. He sometimes forgot parts of his stories and had to use some ploy to fill in the gaps. He also juxtaposed the characters in his stories and frequently misused gender referents (as in "he" for "she"). In addition, there was a certain flatness to his stories: they seem to be reported rather than performed, largely because of a lack of inflection in his delivery. Finally, Packie had a very strong Clare accent and was also very soft spoken. These problems combined so that at times it required tremendous effort simply to attend to his storytelling.[24] (Packie died in June 1990. As Packie was quite old [b. 1903] and infirm at the time that I recorded his tales, it is more than likely that health problems affected his narrating. Unfortunately, I have no examples of his storytelling from earlier periods in his life with which to compare more recent recordings.)

To provide the reader with some experience of these difficulties, I present here the introduction to one of the most structurally complex stories I recorded from Packie, a version of Type 550 (*Search for the Golden Bird*), which I named "The Quarryman's Son." Packie had to endure several kinds of distractions while recounting his tale (the opening and closing of cupboard doors, background conversation and noise, and a number of interruptions), making the transcription to some extent an unfair record of his narrating skills. Nonetheless, I believe it underscores some of the difficulties attendant upon making aesthetic judgments of such narratives.

THE QUARRYMAN'S SON

There was a man and his wife, and they lived close to a quarry pit here in this country. And the only way he had for living was working every day in, in the quarry, selling the gravel. That was the way he was making his living. Anyhow, this time, 'twas in the wintertime, didn't there a great fall of snow come and, by gar, he couldn't go up in the, in the quarry.

"By God," says he to the wife, Maura, says he, "Yer, whatever about the snow," says he, "but sure we'll be hungry," says he, "if we won't have a handful of gravel to sell," says he. "Give me the shovel," says he.

She get the shovel anyway, and he went to see...[unintelligible]...in his quarry and he felt, pelting the shovels of snow till he cleared a way. And, by God, to his great surprise, didn't he see—didn't a door open, and this man opened the door, and he welcomed him.

"By gar," says he, "I be here a long time," says he, "and how, how well you never come *an chuairt* [the visit] to me?" says he.

"I never knew," says the quarryman, "that the likes of you were there."

"Well, they are," says he. "I'm here," says he. "And you haven't any family?"

"No," says he. "How could I expect to have a family? Sure, poor Maura's an old woman now," says he.

"Ah, never mind about that," says the, the giant inside to him. "Your, your wife will have a, a young son," says he, "in less than twelve months time," says he. And he opened a press [cupboard] anyway, and he gave him a big sum of money. "Well, now," says he, "raise that child," says he, "and when he's seven years," says he, "bring him here to me," says he.

"Yes, sure, I will," says poor Sean. Thought that he'd never have a, any family.

So, by gar, 'tis true for him, hadn't they a young son in less than twelve months' time. He grew up to a nice, strong *garsún* [boy], and they had plenty of money. So he was told by the man in the quarry to educate him. So he did, educated him and all.

And when he was seven, that was the bargain, that he should bring him to the man. So he did. And the mother, she was very lonesome after him. So, they get the man of the quarry a great welcome for him—gave him a grand dinner and all. And, "Well, now," says he, "I won't keep [him] today," says he. "He's too young," says he. "Bring him back," says he, "for seven years more," says he. Gave 'em plenty of money—to feed them all and educate the son. Yerra, sure, she was overjoyed when he came home.

He was fourteen years the second time. So, by gar, he brought him then when he was fourteen, and the mother very lonesome after him. "Well now," says the, the quarryman, "I won't keep him today," says he. "Bring him back," says he, "again," says he, "for seven years more, and he'll be twenty-one then," says he, "and he'll be well able to do for himself then," says he.

So he did. Brought him back when he was twenty-one years. And he brought him first when she was seven, then fourteen, and when she was twenty-one then. He was a young man.

"Well now," says he, "I've a lot of money," says he, "lost supporting that boy," says he, "and yourself and your wife," says he. "So," he says, "I'll keep him anymore now, myself," says he, "and, he'll be a rich man," says he. "He'll never be short of anything," says he.

So, by gar, the father, of course, he was very lonesome after him. And when he was comin' home without him, poor Maura—she was an old woman—and she would, didn't she die of grief when he hadn't the son coming back with him.

Very well. He brought in the son, anyhow, and educated him. And, by gar, he got a job for him. And the job was, with this big man, a gentleman, eight or nine clerks with him. And, when the quarryman, when he was passing with him anyhow, he gave him a pen. "Well now," says he, "keep that pen," says he, "and, any letter or anything, anything you have to write," says he, "place the pen in, in, in the paper," says he, "and 'twill write whatever you want," says he.

So, by gar, he did. He got the job with the other nine clerks with this gentleman. And, by gar, he give a prize to the first done, and the best written. So, the quarryman's son got the prize.

By damned, that went on for a while, anyhow, and prior to that, when he was parting from, from his foster father, "Well, now," says he, "you'll travel through this country now," says he, "and it's fine country," says he. And he gave him a bridle. "Go down to that field below," says he, "where there are grand horses there," says he, "and shake the bridle," says he, "bring him here to me," says he.

He did. He went down to the big field where the horses were, and he shook the bridle. Sure, if he did, whatever, the horses, they ran here and there. And he was coming back again, along an avenue that looked into the house, and didn't he see a little pony there.

"Sure, maybe," says he, "you'll stick your head in the, in the bridle." He shook the bridle, and as soon as he did, didn't the little pony stuck his head into the bridle. Yerra, he brought her home then and fed her and took great care of him.

By gar, this was going on—going on for a long time, and the rest of the clerks, they had a meeting, a meeting between themselves.

"Yerra," says the..., "he'll be always very fond of the pony. When he'd be at his work he'd go out to the stable and feed him, give him a drink and all to that."

"Ah, by gar," says the..., "aren't we the good scholars?" says the...They said they were.

"And how is it," says the..., "that man," says he, "the one who was to come up to him," says he, "he's such a scholar?" says he. "And I don't know what's ...[unintelligible]...Maybe 'tis in the pen it is," says he.

So, one of them came in one day, in a hurry, and says, and says the pony was sick outside in the stable. Didn't he run away out, and left the pen in the, in the ink bottle. Yerra, as soon as he went, sure they took the pen, placed it in the, in the paper. Yerra, sure, it wrote away whatever, whatever they'd like.

"Ah," says the man, the boss, says he, "there must be something in that pen," says he. He looked at it. 'Twas a grand pen. "That pen," says he, "belongs to a bird," says he, "they call the 'Golden *Féinics*'" [phoenix].

So now says the boss to him, says he, "Go out," says he now, "and bring that bird here."

"By gar, I don't know," says he.

"Well go," says he.

And he went back to his so-called father, and he told him the story. Well, the father and mother there anyway, they gave him his blessing anyway, and the father said to him, "You'll have to go on horseback today," says he. So they put a grand saddle on the pony, and off he went.

He was travelin' away, anyhow, on his journey, didn't he see a big giant, and he tied up to a big tree....[25]

So begins Packie's long and very complex tale. Packie did manage to develop and resolve the plot, as the full transcription indicates (see Appendix IV), but he became confused at times and was struggling to remember characters or episodes as the story progressed. There were often long pauses between words and phrases, and the ends of many sentences seemed to be suggested rather than articulated, simply fading off. This was particularly true of phrases such as "he says" and "she says," which were sometimes barely audible, and recognizable only because they fit into the logic of the story and Packie's style of narrating. It appeared to be difficult for Packie to sustain speech for very long, which may account for some of these characteristics; it certainly made his willingness to narrate such long stories more noteworthy.

Donal Moore is a true performer, in Hymes' sense, and listening to him is an enjoyable experience. Among the storytellers in English I interviewed, Donal is a superior narrator in terms of plot development and resolution, his use of traditional descriptive language, and the tight, constrained humor of his presentation. His humor is not broad or bombastic; it reveals itself in small things: elements of dialogue, descriptive detail, his vocal inflections. Although Donal uses few gestures and moves very little when he narrates, there is a dramatic quality in his delivery. Some of these characteristics are manifest in this short segment of Donal's tale "The Mac a hAon Fionn" (literally, "The First Son of Fionn"), in which the illegitimate son of Fionn MacCumhail, taunted by playmates for his illegitimacy, goes in search of his father. After losing a wager, the Mac a hAon's quest is to find two ears that were "taken off a king of Ireland long ago." At this juncture in the tale, the Mac a hAon Fionn, with the help of a magic tablecloth, comes to the aid of a farmer who is tyrannized by a "big rancher" whom he must feed for seven years at one sitting.

THE MAC A hAON FIONN

"How is it," he [the Mac a hAon Fionn] says, "that man," he says, "have such an appetite and such a griping desire?"

"Oh, he's a savage man," he said.

"Does he ever do anything bad out of the way," he said, "in this part of the country?"

"Oh, he took the two ears of the king was here long 'go."

"Are you sure he have 'em?"

"I've seen 'em by him," he says.

So, "By God," he says, "that's what I'm out for."

He came anyway [the rancher], about twelve o'clock, and he sat at the table. He had everything and anything put—called from the table for him that he never got below from the farmer.

"You have a grand table," he said.

"Oh, I am—I have," he says.

"Is that a little Irish fellow there," he says, "sitting in the hearth?"

"Oh, yes, it is," he said.

"God," he said, "'tis long 'go," he says, "I took the top of the two ears off a king," he says, "in Ireland," he says. "And look, Paddy," he says to the farmer, "they're as fresh as ever."

The farmer looked at him. "I never seen 'em," says the farmer.

"God," says Mac a hAon Fionn, "I'd love to see 'em." Do you see?

"Yerra, what do you want seeing 'em, you *créatur*?" he says.

"Well, I'd like to see 'em."

"Well, I suppose," says the farmer, "we—Do you mind that we have a look at 'em?"

He gave 'em to them, and the Mac a hAon put 'em down in a little pocket and walked out the door....[26]

Donal renders many details of the tale very humorously. The amusing effect of his use of inflection is best illustrated by the questioning of the farmer by the landlord concerning the Mac a hAon Fionn ("Is that a little Irish fellow...sitting in the hearth?"). Donal's voice here is very high and small, an effect that simply cannot be conveyed except in the hearing. The freshness of the king's ears shows Donal's light comic touch. Examples of his style elsewhere in the story include his assessment of the Mac a hAon's size ("He was classified small to be a giant") and his description of the powers of the magic tablecloth ("I have gifted grub here"). One must recall that Donal originally narrated his tales solely in Irish and later started telling them in English. Undoubtedly the quality of his diction derives at least in part from the fact that he is translating these tales from the Irish.

John Campbell is the youngest person I met with any command of traditional storytelling, although he currently narrates in a number of settings that are not really conducive to the telling of long, complex stories: on television, on the radio, at musical gatherings such as *Comhaltas Ceoltóirí Éireann* (Brotherhood of Irish Musicians) sessions in Forkhill.[27] John does not have Donal's command of the descriptive detail typical of traditional stories, nor are his plots so detailed. However, the motivations of the characters in his stories are clear and the plots are maintained and resolved. His presentations are dramatic in the more modern sense of that word—relative to Donal's, for instance—but not histrionic. Their dramatic quality is achieved more through gesture and the vocal qualities of his narrating. His shorter, humorous stories and his style of narrating are popular among a wider audience than is typical of traditional storytellers. He has been influenced by Eamon Kelly, among others, and is a storyteller in the more modern vein.[28]

The following is a segment of John's tale "Above and Beyond the End of the Earth," an amalgam of several international tale types.[29] The theme and characters are the familiar ones of the quest of the unpromising younger son assisted by a supernatural (animal) helper. (The complete transcription can be found in Appendix IV.) John's diction in his tales is actually more modern than either Donal's or Packie's, but he makes full use of dialectal elements typical of south Armagh (particularly "wee" for "little") which make his language both colorful and reminiscent of the past.

ABOVE AND BEYOND THE END OF THE EARTH

There was a king in Ireland, and he had three sons. And one of them was a devil-may-care fella, and he went away. And he went to France. And he gadded about in France, uh, and spent all his money. And, uh, eventually, he come back home. And when he come back home, the very day he arrived back home, his father was after being buried.

And the other two sons, when he went into the castle, the other two sons was in the countin' room, dividin' the money. And the minute they saw him, they said, "Where are you going?"

He says. "I'm back home."

"You know father's dead?"

"No, I didn't know that. What are yous doing with the money?"

"We're dividin' it. He left it all between us."

"Did you not leave any for me?"

"No. All he left you is the low meadow—the low, long meadow—down by the river." You see.

So, he was very—he was very disappointed. And, uh, after a day or two, he said to himself, "Well, I better go down and see this land that I got in the low, long meadow down by the river."

And down he went, and when he looked into the meadow, there was three horses in the meadow. And, one of them had a little foal. But the foal was only about the size of a rabbit—a wee, delicate, puny foal. So, he says to himself, "Lord, three fine horses there, and that foal with the spindly legs running after it and..." You know. "I think I'll drown that foal in the river. Going to—not going to waste grass an, an, and a good mare on, that animal."

So he went out and he caught the foal, and he was draggin' the foal down to put it into the river. And when he got to the brow of the river, the foal spoke to him. And he says, "Ah, don't drown me. Give me one chance," he says. "Maybe," he says, "when I get runnin' about and gets the good flush of grass," he says, "I might grow into a big fine colt."

So, he looked at him, and he says, "Well, you're entitled to one chance." And he let him go.

And he went away to France for another twelve months. And after the twelve months he come back again, and when he went down to the low, long meadow beside the, the river, the foal was still there and it didn't grow any bigger. And he was mad. And he crossed into the field, and he caught the wee foal, and he was taking it down to drowned it. And when the wee foal got down to the other river, he says, "I just want one request. There's a saddle," he says, "under the bushes, and will you just take it over and put it on me back, so as I'll have to say when I go in the world—into the world beyond, that there was harness on me back."

So, the man went over. And when he went over there, there was a saddle and bridle and everything where the wee foal told him it was. And he took it over, and he said, "I'll not put it on your back. It'll break...."

"No," he says, "put it on my back." So, he put it on his back.

He says, "Tighten the girt!" And, he tightened the girt.

And when he tightened the girt on the sa, on the saddle, the foal grew into a great big, big horse. Lovely big, black horse.

"Now," he says, "get up on my back," he says, "and I'll, and I'll give you a ride before you drowned me." And he went round the meadow like the wind.

And, uh, the man was all enchanted. "Well," he says, "ah, I'll not the devil to drowned," he says, "I'll do on you," he says. "I'll tell you what. I'm sorry," he says, "but I've to go 'way to France. You stay where—I'll leave the saddle on you," he says, "till I come back."

He says, "Sure, what's taking you to France? I'll take you to France," he says. "You sit where you are."

"Oh," he says, "you couldn't...."

"Oh," he says, "I could take you to France. You just sit where you are, and I'll take you to France."

So he galloped along like the wind. And he galloped along the sea. And he's gallopin' on, and he come to a place where there was a wee, low bridge—humpy-back bridge. And the horse turned 'round, and he says to him, "Now, when I—when we cross this bridge," he says, "don't you speak anymore," he says, "till I land you in France, because if you do," he says, "something'll happen."

So on they galloped along the sea, and it come on dark. And out in the sea, the king's son in the saddle, he saw this thing shinin'. And it grew, and it grew, and it grew, and it grew into a big light. He thought the sea was on fire. And he says to himself, "I wonder what that be." Out loud, like that.

And just with that the horse says, "Damn you for opening your mouth!" he says. "I'll have to swim out there now."

And he swam out. And when he got away out to where this light was, it started to get smaller and smaller until it was just like a silver thread. But it was shinin' in the water. The horse says, "I'm going to swim round in a circle now," he says, "and you put out your hand and catch that," he says. "And the minute you catch it," he says, "put it into your inside pocket."

So, he galloped 'round, and he put out his hand and he caught it, and he put it into his inside pocket. He says, "For that's a hair out of the head of the Queen of Sleepy Island." So, he put it in his pocket, and he thought nothing of it.

And the next thing, they landed in France. And they went up to the King of France, and up he went, and a servant come and took the horse, and they put the horse into a stable. And, he got down, do you see, and shook his clothes. Shook his coat and put it on him again to look a bit respectable goin' in to the King of France.

And when they went in, they were sittin' talkin', and they sat by the window. And all of a sudden the King of France says, "My stables are on fire!" The whole place was lit up.

And they ran out. And when they went down, the hair had fell out of his pocket, and 'twas lyin' on the stable and it had the whole stable lit up. So, he put down his hand to catch it, to lift it to put it in his pocket, and the King says, "Show me that!" And the king says, "That's the hair," he says, "out of the head of the Queen of Sleepy Island. So you know where she is," he says, "and I'm going to order you now," he says, "to go and fetch her here first light in the mornin'...."[30]

Breaking the interdiction on speech signals the inevitable quest, and the hero goes off to fetch the Queen of Sleepy Island.

Many of the stories of the other narrators I interviewed during this research would come under the category of *scéalaíocht*, but the narrators are less accomplished than the aforementioned storytellers. Francie Kennelly is typical. Although he can tell some long and complexly structured tales, his diction while narrating is almost that of ordinary speech; it does not evoke the "otherworldly" quality of the folktale through those formulaic openings (or closings) that establish what Nicolaisen calls "narrative time": that time "which sets the general time frame of the story apart from historical time."[31] (Even though traditional storytelling in English is less stylized than that in Irish, it has elements which are recognizably peculiar to it. These include formulaic openings and closings and elaborate use of both direct and indirect speech.[32]) During our interview Francie seemed to be rushing through his stories, and he paid only moderate attention to the incorporation of descriptive detail.[33] Mrs. Droney could tell several international folktales, but her development of both structural and content elements, as well as the psychological side of these tales (including motivation and character development), was decidedly minimal. The same can be said, in varying degrees, of Patrick O'Farrell, Martin McKenna, Jack Mahony, and Junior Crehan.

I include here a short excerpt from Francie Kennelly's tale, "The Gentlemen's Agreement," which is a version of an international folktale on the familiar theme of a bargain with the devil (Type 1178, *The Devil Outriddled*); it includes elements from a number of other international tale types. As in this example, Francie characteristically localizes his tales by incorporating details familiar to those who live in this area of Clare (Miltown Malbay).

THE GENTLEMEN'S AGREEMENT

Out there in Spanish Point—I suppose you know it? [CH: Yes, I do.] Couple of hundred yards now, where the president of Ireland was born. [CH: Hillery.] Yes, Doctor Paddy Hillery. There was a man living there, and he had a big family. He had eight or nine in, in family. Boys and girls and every way. But they immigrated, some of 'em. They went to Australia, and they went to America, and they went every place. He was only a small farmer. He had the place of a cow and a mule. That's all he had.

But he was a road contractor as well. Uh, he used to make four miles of a road, like. And the money, the adopted money that was over the four miles of a road, was seventeen pounds thirteen and four pence. But he had this—she had this boy at home, and there was a couple of girls there. He was a great boy. He was a football kicker, and he was a mighty worker. 'Twas he used trim the roads. The roads had to be trimmed. The lough spits had to be trimmed. He had to break two hundred yards of stones and put 'em out in what they called recesses, and spread 'em at the end of the year. But he was well able for it. 'Twas no trouble in the world to him to break three yards of stones in a day.

Well, he, what they call—They had what they call that time a "neddy hammer." There was a twelve ounce and an eight ounce neddy in it. And you see, if you were breakin' heavy stones, you'd have the twelve ounce neddy. And if you're breakin' the lighter stones, do you see, you'd have the, the other....[CH: Different—different ends.] Yes. Yeah. But, uh....[CH: What is it called again?] A neddy hammer. A neddy. Well—I don't know how now is that the right name, but that's the name they were called. But, 'twas no bother to this boy. He used do terrible work. They used rise seaweed as well and make kelp. And they had a great stumble of a black [back?] garden.

But, things were, things were going according to plan. Indeed they were. They were kind of all right. There was a bit of money coming from America, and this was a great boy. The money of the road was coming in, and they had the milk of the cow, and all that.

But this day, in the month of July, he was breakin' stones, and he was never going as good. He was stripped to the shirt now, a grand warm day, and he was, he was thinkin' that he'd beat the three yards that day—that he'd break more, he was goin' so well. This fine girl passed now, as fine as a man ever looked at. And a lot of people used pass Spanish Point. 'Twas a holiday resort even that time. 'Twas all English was here like, and...he was surprised, this girl, she said, "God bless the work!"[34]

"God," he said, "that's strange anyway. On you too," says he.

But she walked down the road in front of him. And he looked after her, and he thought she was the finest girl he ever saw. No more bother now in the world to her, to—Miss Ireland or Miss Universe. Any of them things would be no more bother to her, she was such a fine girl.

She went away, anyway. And he was breakin' away, but I suppose he was thinkin' of the girl away. Naturally enough. And this man came. A fine looking man. A grand suit of clothes. A tailor-made suit and a grand pair of brown shoes. And a Duffy hat. They were in style at the time. Collar and tie and all. Dressed, dressed grand. Well, he didn't say "God bless the work," but he spoke to him.

But, they were talking for a start anyway, and he said to him—But the young fella that was breakin' the stones noticed one thing about him, that he had very, very dangerous eyes. Shifty, kind of dangerous eyes. He was giving him the white of the eye a little bit. But, uh, they spoke for a start anyway, and he, this man said to him, "I saw you looking at that grand girl that passed," said he.

"Oh God," says the young fellow, "why wouldn't anyone?"

"Well, listen," says he, "in two hours time," says he, "make up your mind, and I'll put you—I'll, I'll get you to marry that girl," says he. By God, the young fellow was thinking in himself anyway.

"I'll be back in two hours now," says he. "But one condition," says he, "that you must sell your soul."

By God, sure, he put the young fellow thinkin'. He was thinkin' of the grand girl.

"She's very well off, too," says he. "She has a mighty farm of land and the world of money."

The fella did come back in two hours, and I suppose the young fella was rippin' knots, and the girl came back again. Walkin' this way, like—against him. Whatever way she looked, the time before, she was ten times better looking this time.

By God, anyway, your man landed—the, the devil. He was the devil, do you see? He was dressed, dressed in civilian's clothes. Now all the pictures you saw of the devil, he had a pair of horns and a tail, didn't he? But not this time. He was dressed in civilian's clothes, beautiful clothes. By God, they were....

"Have you my—an answer ready for me?" he said to the young fella.

"Give me a chance," said the young fella. "Give me another hour," he said.

He came back again in another hour, and damn it, wasn't the young fella tempted, and didn't he, didn't he sign on with him.

"Okay," says the devil, says he, "be here," says he, "tomorrow, again," says he. "We'll have no writin' drawn, but we'll, we'll settle it up," says he. "You'll, you'll give me your word," says he. "You're word is your bond," says he, "today ten years I can claim your soul," he said.

"Okay", says the fella.

There was—'twas a gentleman's agreement. They shook hands. They shook hands like that. 'Twas a gentleman's agreement. And 'twas a deal anyway.[35]

Eventually the devil comes to reclaim the soul, but agrees to a riddling contest and is outriddled and defeated. (The complete transcription can be found in Appendix IV.) As I noted, Francie's diction here is really that of ordinary conversation. A comparison of Francie's narrating with those of the other narrators discussed above reveals considerable differences in style of language, rhythm, and tone.

The English Language Tradition: Narrating and Narrators of *Seanchas*

The judgment of what constitutes a good *seanchaí* is much more flexible than that regarding the *scéalaí* because there are fewer formal criteria for stories in this category.[36] *Seanchas* characteristically does not include the formulaic descriptive passages associated with hero tales. Also, because these tales are generally shorter and often mono-episodic, that ability to build episode upon episode, which is so prized in the telling of *scéalaíocht*, is less important for the narrating of *seanchas*.[37] (A certain degree of control over structure is always expected in storytelling; this is what gives experience "story" form.) In the strict sense the *seanchaí* is a historian, but this category of narrative also includes stories about encounters with ghosts, fairies, or any kind of "supernatural" being (themes with which Irish tradition abounds), and the recounting of personal or unusual experiences of all kinds. Virtually anyone who wishes may tell such stories.

The narrators of *seanchas* also display a wide range of capabilities. Perhaps the least competent as a *seanchaí* is Mick O'Brien, to whom I was directed by Francie Kennelly. Although Mr. O'Brien knows lots of anecdotes about local happenings, he does not elaborate his stories structurally or linguistically in any way. They are clearly reported rather than performed. Jacko McGann was a good narrator of *seanchas*, although he never considered himself a storyteller.[38] Junior Crehan's telling of *seanchas* is far superior to his telling of *scéalaíocht*, at least among the tales that I recorded from him. His shorter stories are interesting and amusing and he seems to be more involved in telling them.

Junior's telling of a tale I have called "The Fairy Football Match" was a true performance.[39] It contains many traditional motifs associated with fairies and, although I recorded many stories about personal experiences with fairies or "fairy phenomena," it is the only purely humorous one. It is illustrative of Junior's drollery and, in a sense, his gentleness—qualities for which he is known. The tale is relatively short, and I present it here in its entirety.

THE FAIRY FOOTBALL MATCH

Yerra, a thing happened to myself one time. Course, as you know, I was travelin' the country, fiddlin'. Dances, I'd be called. Dance here and dance there.

So there was a lad home here from America. He often played with me—dances—before he went. So, my father and myself were making a cock of hay over there, and 'twas kind of a bad harvest, too. And your man pulled up over in the road, and he was hootin' the car. "Go down," he says. "He must be someone that's looking for a road or something." So, I went down. Shook hand to him...[unintelligible]....

"There's a bit of a dance at the house tonight. You go over," he said.

"I will," says I, anyhow. "I promised about a house back here, but I'll go some time in the night, Tom," said I to him.

"Good," he said. "I'm going for a few bottles of whiskey and things," he said. So I came back anyway.

"Who is it?" said my father.

"Tom Looney's home," says I.

"I suppose he wants you tonight."

"He does," says I.

"Well, go if you like," he said, "but I'll be calling you at seven in the morning." Be woke. Oh, the old people were strict. When they had work to do you be at home, and you had to do it. "I'll be calling you. We're doing the oats tomorrow," he says, "at seven o'clock."

But, anyway, I went back to the dance. And I had to cross a field where there was a fort—a *ráth*—and it had a very lonesome name. So, I, yer' I got plenty of drink that, over at that house, and I told the man of the house, "I have to go now," I said, "at twelve o'clock tonight."

"Alone?" he said.

"Ah, there's a bit of a night there. Only I promised both of you."

"Well, I'm very thankful to you," said he, "you have a lot done."

"There was a few more musicians there, see, and they'll keep you going."

I left anyway, but, and I comin' in, in this field where the *ráth* was, and there'd a kind of fog come, you know. *Ceo* [fog], we call it. 'Twouldn't, 'twouldnt wet you but 'twas....[CH: Misty, kind of...] Misty, yes. So, there was a step going in, and I stood up on the step. Then I saw all the little men in the, hurlin' the ball. And 'twas like a, the ball it was like a bulb. 'Twas like...[CH: Like a light, a light bulb.] Yeah. 'Twas the light from going across through the fog. And when they came off of the wall anyway, and they had a goal post. But, uh, this ball came and didn't it hit me in the side of the leg, and roll back again.

So, the little man that was in the goal, "Oh, God!" says he, "you done a great turn for me. If that goal went out I'd be in terrible trouble. There'd be a penance put on me," says he.

So, I don't know why I stopped at all, but I'd a terrible pain in my leg for a week after. So, your—the referee blew the whistle and they all cleared. I suppose in the fort. And your little man didn't go in at all. He walked with me.

"How is it you didn't go inside with them?"

"Ah, I'm a different breed," he said. "I'm the *Dristín Luachra*. I live in the rushes." That was his home. "And I'll give you an advice," he said. "If you're traveling through the land by night, avoid the rushes! Avoid the patch of rushes! You might get into trouble."

So he was coming away with me, and "*An bhfuil tú pósadh?* Are you married?"

"No."

"And would you like to get married?"

"Sure, I would and I wouldn't. Sure, I have a grand old time," I said, "single."

"Well," he said, "I'll give you something now," he said. "Any girl you want," he says, "you can have her."

He give me a little thing like a horseshoe nail, about that length. Do you know the nail for driving a horseshoe? 'Twas like gold, and it was wrapped up in tinsel.

"You told me you were going to another dance," he said.

"I am," said I.

"Are you afraid of me?" he said.

"I amn't," I said, "no."

"So, if you see a girl at that dance that you want to have," said he, "she's up on the floor dancin', put that," says he, "under the strings of your fiddle, and play for her, and nothing in the world," says he, "will take her from you. But one thing I'll warn you, don't bring it in under the roof of any house until you go into that dance. If you do," says he, "'tis no good to you."

So I stole in here, anyway. I had an old, bad string on the fiddle, and I had strings there in the press [cupboard]. And I said I'd come in for the string. Never thought of what he told me, and I was just going to open the door when I heard the voice, "Stop the ball!"

"Cripes!" says I. I took it out of my pocket and I left it in the window and I came in and I got, yerra, three or four strings, and I stuck in my pocket and brought the little yoke and went over.

Dance was goin' on. Poor woman below was up, dancin' on the floor, dancin' a jig, and I puts this behind, and anything like the music was never heard. They were all kind of in a, a kind of doze. All the people. And when I left up the fiddle she was sittin' on my knees. And that's how that happened. That's a fact. [CH: That's a wonderful story. Did you ever have to give it back?] Disappeared. Disappeared. [CH: And that was it?] Didn't need a second wife.[40]

In my estimation, John Reilly is a superlative *seanchaí*. I believe he is consciously presenting the tradition. His tales incorporate many themes well attested in the tradition but unique among the storytellers I recorded, such as the ability to foretell imminent death through the vision of a supernatural funeral, the gifts of the seventh son, and tales of priests triumphing over Protestant landlords. His stories convey a broad knowledge of traditional folkways and evince his strong interest in all aspects of rural life. They are full of interesting digressions and, at times, an extraordinary degree of detail.

The subjective experience of listening to John narrate was also exceptional. He brought a degree of intensity to his performance that I did not encounter in any other storyteller: speaking quickly, moving around the room, and gesticulating a great deal. (Jack Mahony's presence may have accounted partially for this.) There is also a soft, more "feminine" quality to the things that John notices and describes. During our conversation about his previous house, he commented at length on the colors of the flowers surrounding the house and the singing of the little birds in the trees—types of subjects upon which the men to whom I talked in Ireland did not usually elaborate. He is completely involved in his narrating and is thoroughly entertaining.

John's story about "Felix," which I present here in full, is unusual in the body of material I recorded about fairies and their relationships to humans in that it involves a number of incidents, rather than a central event, and it describes an on-going relationship with the entity Felix. Although the basic import of the tale is frightening, for Felix attempts to kill a local man, the story has many comical details: the image of Felix on the turkey cock riding under the cow; Felix drinking the cow's milk; Felix liking the name "Felix." John's description of the spinning wheel attests to his interest in traditional technology, a recurrent characteristic of his storytelling.

FELIX

There was another house in the locality. You know the one—this house now, Jack, that I'm going talking about [Jack Mahony is present]. Coyne's house. Well, that was another thatched house. Well, they left that house because it was haunted. There was ghosts in it, you see. And, when I was a, a young lad about twelve or fourteen, I used to go in and out, you see, occasionally.

So there was a little man in it, and he was about eighteen inches high. A—a ghost. And he used to travel around, a-ridin' in a turkey cock. That was his transport. And, in this—this was a fact, you know. They had to leave the house. And this little man was about that high. And he, he wore knick—little knickerbockers. You know them, with the...[CH: The kind that bundle up around here?] Yes. And there was little buttons down there, look. And, a little whip. You know, about that size. And a little wizened little face, you know. Not pretty or anything. And, uh, he had this turkey cock, and he'd hop on, on the—The little chair at the back of the turkey cock was built up this way. He used to lean back on it, and the turkey cock'd fly from one tree to the other, about sixty feet up.

But that—When they left the house and went to the new *tigh* [house], that disappeared and never was seen since. Like, the house was haunted. They lived ever in it, until they left it.

And, I was there one day, and there was like a little loft up here in the house. And they were eatin' their dinner at the table. And I was at this big, open fire. You know them sort? You know, with the kettle on the hob? And the, the cat around in the hob, you know, and him washing his face, you know. And, and, socks and everything hung on the crane? That—You know the crane? [CH: Yes, the thing that hung down over the fireplace?] Yes. Well, I was sittin' there, and there was a grand—the poor old woman—and she came over and gave me some grub. I was a little lad about that size. So I was eatin' the grub. And there was—you know what turf is? And the turf used to be fired down on the table, down from this loft. And the old man used to take the sod of turf and throw it in the fire, that way. And he'd keep eatin', eatin' away, and another sod down. But I tell you I was a young lad. I kept my eye on the loft and could not see a thing in the loft. Nothing. Yes. So, finally, before they got up from the table, the little man hopped down on a box—and he wasn't much bigger than the tape recorder there—and out the backdoor. So, that was that for that day like. They didn't know—wonder a bit. They were used to it.

So, anyhow, anyhow, after I was there again. It was a few days after I was passin', and I was talking to this old man—man. He was a nice old man. And the old woman. And there was a—also the young man and his wife. So, we were talking away. And she was spinning with that wooden wheel, making the thread. And the—the young woman had these yokes, and carvin' [?]. Did you see them? [CH: No, I haven't. What are they exactly?] There two of yokes about a foot—about the size of that. About—about eight inches by a foot. And there was a handle there on it. And there was steel wire—like a wire, steel wire brush. And you'd hold one there, and you'd, you'd leave a bit of work, and you'd tease the wool that way. And you'd—just break the wool like that, and you'd feed it into the wheel, and spin the wheel, and 'twould make a lovely thread.

So the old woman was spinning, you see, and I happened to look over the garden, and there the man was with the, the turkey cock, and he hopped out through bushes. And, the cows—you know, they had cows, for milkin', you know. And there was two cows. And he walked under the cow. And he was only—Oh, he could walk cross, back and over, under the cow. And he put up his mouth, and there he started milking the cow like that. And he—he had all the milk drank off—out of the cows. And the cow would not kick in a hundred years. You know, a cow...[CH: The cow had that much sense, I suppose.] No, the cow liked him. And, the cow—a cow, you know, she rechews. You know what that means? When a cow eats for two hours she has two stomachs. And, that's gone down in that stomach. She lies down then, and she'll settle herself, and she'd get a nice dry spot in the field. And when she lies down she start doing this. Chewing her cud. That's the meaning of that. She brings that up out of that stomach, rechews it, and lets it down in this one. Well, she was there, and that man-ín at, at her, and she was chewin' her cud. Like that. And she used to have her eyes half shut. She liked it that good. Whatever he was doin', she liked—she did like it. And, that was the gamut.

So we followed him—a few young lads, we followed him and fired stones after him—bricks or anything. And you couldn't hit him, if you died. And we called him every name, and the only name he fancied calling him was "Felix." He, he, he used turn back and look when you'd say "Felix," don't you know. [CH: How long was he around now? How long did he stay around?] He was there at the time, but when they left and went to the new *tigh*, that ended that.

So, anyhow, I'll tell you really now. There was brothers that came home from England. You know. Great big men. And they were used to be two of 'em, and they—maybe in wintertime, you know? They'd stay for a month or two and go back again.

So this man was at home. And he was a in bed in the room in the old thatched house, you see, at night. And they went to bed. They were in the one bed actually, himself and the brother. And, the brother woke up, the fella that was at home, and he heard an awful noise. He woke up, and he listened around the room like this, don't you know. And, uh, he says, uh....He stirred and shook the sleep off himself, you know. And, he turned around, and there was the brother. And the noise—the brother was chokin'. And when he looked at the brother, the little man was in the bed. And, you know a towel for drying yourself? Not a big towel now. He had the hand towel within in his mouth, and him pushing down, down, down. And your man was asleep. And, he started to choke. And, he kept chokin', and chokin'. And only for the other brother wakin' in the meantime, and he made a dive for the man-ín...[unintelligible]...[41] And the man-ín jumped onto a table, and he went up a hole in a loft. You couldn't catch him if you dived, he was that quick. But in the meantime, he made for the brother. And there was about that much out of the towel. And he pulled, and pulled, and pulled until the last bit of the towel came out. And he pressed him like that. [CH: To make him breathe, I suppose.] And he did breathe. And he woke up.

He said, "What's wrong?" he said.

"You may thank...," he says, "that I wakened," he said, "or you would have gone to the next world." [CH: He was thankful for his brother, I'm sure.] Yes, he was awful thankful to him. He says, "I'll be at Ballyhaunis station tomorrow, and I'll go to England," he said. "I'll tell you," he says, "the little man won't catch me in a hurry again," don't you know.[42]

Because the telling of *seanchas*—stories such as Junior's and John's above—does not make the same demands on a narrator in terms of the manipulation of plot structures and the use of more formulaic language that the narrating of *scéalaíocht* frequently does, individuals are more willing to step into the role of "traditional storyteller" as *seanchaí* than *scéalaí*. This applies to several narrators discussed in this study who began to think of themselves as "storytellers" after having had some of their stories recorded by a folklore collector (e.g., Frank Anderson, Patrick O'Farrell, and Elizabeth Bourke); it is simply easier to tell stories of this kind. Furthermore, the contemporary public generally has little, if any, exposure to the tradition of narrating *scéalaíocht*, and there is no popular demand for storytelling of this kind. The length of most *seanchas* is also more in line with the expectations conditioned by popular contemporary media, such as radio and television, and so it is usually the tellers of *seanchas* who find themselves on programs that seek to present aspects of Irish "traditional" (i.e., rural) life to the urban public. Because these stories are less arcane and require less knowledge of the tradition for their enjoyment, the public is more accepting of traditional storytelling in this vein.

FINAL CONSIDERATIONS AND PORTENTS OF CHANGE

An issue that I wish to address here, because it is related to the synergy of scholars and the storytelling tradition and to the larger issue of the public's perception of traditional storytelling, is that of the declining *social* significance of the terms *scéalaí* and *seanchaí*. Éamonn Ó Donnghaile, a narrator of stories in Irish, lives in the *Gaeltacht* area of Carna, Co. Galway, which has always been considered one of the richest in traditional lore in Ireland.[43] Éamonn discussed with me the important social distinctions between the roles associated with the two branches of the storytelling tradition which were adhered to locally. According to Éamonn, a *seanchaí* in the strict sense was a historian. He was expected to be learned in local history and genealogical lore and to be committed to the accuracy of his information. In this role the *seanchaí* was not a "storyteller." There was no leeway allowed for embellishment or for what Éamonn calls "the second version" of any actual event.[44] The *scéalaí* was the "storyteller." He was not bound by this commitment to accuracy and was free to embellish within the limits prescribed by the tradition.[45] A *seanchaí* might also be a *scéalaí*, and vice versa, but a good storyteller was expected to abide by the prescriptions associated with either role.

It was Éamonn's opinion that some of the collectors for the Irish Folklore Commission working in the area had blurred the distinctions between these two types of narrators by failing to realize that they were recording material from individuals who were not accepted locally as either *scéalaí* or *seanchaí*. According to Éamonn, there were several narrators in the area who were not committed to the ideals of the tradition but who could patch together a good story from bits and pieces of other tales. Their stories were referred to as *rámhaille* (literally, "delirium," "raving," "a foolish statement").[46] Whatever their skills as entertainers, these narrators were not considered true *seanchaí* or *scéalaí*. By recording historically inaccurate material from inferior *seanchaí* who did not feel bound to the ideal of complete accuracy, the collectors were allowing these narrators the leeway traditionally accorded only to *scéalaí*; they were not abiding by the traditional distinctions.

Éamonn's comments on this subject made me realize, first, that these terms represented concrete realities and were not merely conventional categories of folklore scholarship and, second, that the differences in the meaning of these terms and the social roles they entailed were strictly maintained at the local level in Carna, at least in Éamonn's perception. I then became interested in the question of how rigidly such distinctions had or had not been maintained in other *Gaeltacht* areas.[47] I discussed Éamonn's views on this subject with four others whom I considered potentially knowledgeable on this subject: Cáit O'Sullivan and Donal Moore, both narrators in Irish; Michael O'Connell, a former schoolteacher living in Cahirsiveen (Co. Kerry); and Seán Ó Duinnín in Coolea (in the Cork *Gaeltacht*).[48] These discussions were not very fruitful, for none of them attributed the importance to these distinctions that Éamonn did.[49] This suggested to me that Éamonn's views were either basically idiosyncratic, or they were an accurate characterization solely of the tradition in Carna, the area with which he is most familiar. However, the fact that my questions on this subject did not strike the others with whom I discussed it as especially meaningful and elicited only vague responses at least hinted that the traditional distinctions embodied in these terms are no longer as important in Ireland, or in the storytelling tradition, as they may have been at one time.

Whether or not the terms *scéalaí* and *seanchaí* ever had any general currency with those who were not involved in, or familiar with, traditional storytelling is difficult to ascertain. If it is true that there has been a diminution in the former significance of these terms, Eamon Kelly has undoubtedly contributed to it by appropriating some of the meaning of *scéalaí* in his use of *seanchaí*. As I have noted (in the Introduction), in the general population in Ireland the term *seanchaí* has become the term generally used to refer to any storyteller whose tales are conceived of as "traditional." This is primarily because of the popularity of Eamon Kelly's storytelling and his adaptation of the persona of the "shanachie," the rural storyteller, in his various media performances. Many of Kelly's stories are, in fact, adaptations of traditional narratives, but many are tales that would be told by a *scéalaí*, not a *seanchaí*. But Kelly is not a historian. His popularization of this word has created an image and a meaningful point of reference for many individuals who had no prior knowledge of the storytelling tradition, of these two terms, or of the distinctions between them. I rarely heard the term *scéalaí* used in Ireland, even by folklorists; but "The Shanachie" was used to refer to Eamon Kelly in almost every conversation in which I had reason to discuss my purpose there. It was also used by several of the narrators to refer to "storytellers." The public's familiarity with and acceptance of this word may, in fact, be influencing scholars to use it in much the same way, at least in contexts that do not demand further clarification or refinement of meaning. This is the "complaint" that was at the root of Éamonn Ó Donnghaile's comments on the collectors in Carna. Because the traditional functions associated with both kinds of storytelling continue to have less and less social importance at the local level, these terms *may* eventually become purely academic distinctions.

There are several other issues related to the ways in which the storytelling tradition has been regarded and treated by Irish folklore scholars. As I have observed, the differential interest and status accorded the tradition in Irish blurs both the importance of the interplay between the two language traditions and the complexity of the situation regarding the decline of the language as it is reflected in the lives of individuals. The fact is that the narrators of stories in *both* languages interviewed for this study represent a tremendous diversity of experience with the Irish language. Both Katie Droney (now deceased) and Peter Kelleher usually narrated in English but had learned a number of children's stories (as children) that they could narrate in either language. Although Elizabeth Bourke now narrates in English, she was a fluent Irish speaker until she stopped speaking the language some time after her marriage in 1915. Some of the local legends that she tells are stories she originally heard in Irish. Martin McKenna has lived all his life in an area of Clare (the adjacent villages of Murrough and Fanore) which was completely Irish speaking until very recently. Although he understands Irish perfectly and Irish-language narratives were the models for some of his stories, he does not now speak Irish and has always narrated in English. Donal Moore's stories are tales he currently narrates in both languages.

Not only have traditional narratives crossed over "linguistic boundaries," but they have crossed "media boundaries" as well. My interviews revealed numerous interesting and complex examples. Máirtín Lenihan, a narrator of stories in Irish from whom I recorded several English-language narratives, learned a number of international folktales from a local man in Gleninagh (Co. Clare), Martin Nestor.[50] Nestor was "an educated man" who originally read printed versions of these stories in English and then went on to tell them in his own Irish. Seán Ó Duinnín always narrates in Irish, but the original sources of some of his traditional stories are printed versions he read in English and then "put his own Irish on." As I noted in the Introduction, many of the storytellers learned tales from school texts or recitations in both languages which involved the important figures of the heroic cycles (particularly CúChulainn and Fionn MacCumhail). (Few continued to tell these stories as adults, however, perhaps because the original renderings were at a very basic linguistic level or because the storytellers themselves no longer had children in their own homes for whom such stories were suitable.) When viewed in terms of the complexity of individual experience, then, the situation regarding the decline of the language is not unilinear, but multifaceted, kaleidoscopic. If it is true, as Patrick Ford asserts, that "language is the first context in which we view culture and the single most important context [for a tradition],"[51] then the study of the ways in which the social and cognitive realms represented by these two languages interact and diverge, and the relationship of this divergence to the process of narrating, would offer much to the understanding of modern Ireland as well as to folktale scholarship.

The situation in Ireland today regarding traditional storytelliing in both languages is very complex, but this is particularly true of traditional storytelling in the English language. Among scholars, it is clear that the tradition in English has received less attention than that in Irish; and certainly the English-language narrators receive fewer accolades or laurels. At the Department of Irish Folklore (University College, Dublin) collecting activity for its own sake has decreased in recent years because of the tremendous backlog of material that still remains to be catalogued and made available for use in the archives, and the recognition on the part of scholars that something more must be done with all this material.[52] It is worth very little if it is not used; it requires some analysis and explication.

Although *folklore* in Ireland has been conceived of primarily as the study of survivals (i.e., of the remnants from earlier stages of cultural development), contemporary Irish scholars do recognize that there are modern forms of folklore. Work is being done there in this area, particularly on urban belief tales. The Irish scholars dealing with these materials realize that such legends are contemporary, realistic, and literally global in distribution.[53] There is an implicit tension in this recognition, however. Once it is acknowledged that "new" forms of folklore can develop, it must ultimately be recognized, however unwillingly, that "tradition" is as much an interpretive process as "an inherited body of customs and beliefs," and that it is being "created" all the time.[54] This awareness bodes well for the storytelling tradition in English in its totality, for Irish scholars for the first time are virtually being forced to evaluate examples of modern folklore (i.e., narratives) according to criteria that are *not* derived from the aesthetic canons of traditional storytelling in

Irish. It must then become harder for scholars to justify *conceptually* the continued emphasis on narrative and other traditional materials in the Irish language and the continued neglect of those in English. It is simply untenable to continue to regard English as anything less than a second vernacular language and not to recognize the long-standing, parallel tradition represented in the English-language materials. The need for a broader conceptual framework for the study of tradition is a very basic problem that Irish folklore scholars must eventually address.

A second phenomenon that may exert some influence on Irish traditional storytelling in English is that of the international storytelling revival. The revival began in the United States in the early 1970s, and the number of storytellers utilizing traditional tales from diverse traditions (including Irish stories) has been growing steadily ever since. The National Association for the Preservation and Perpetuation of Storytelling (NAPPS), whose headquarters are in Tennessee, produces a very sophisticated array of publications and is in the process of building up a large national archive on oral storytelling. Its national directory, published yearly, list publications for professional storytellers, storytelling organizations, and storytelling events all over the United States and in a number of foreign countries, including Canada, Venezuela, Germany, and Northern Ireland. NAPPS also has an impressive catalogue of records, tapes, and publications of stories and on storytelling available to both storytellers and the general public. Despite the rapidity and breadth of the growth of interest in oral storytelling, American folklorists as a whole are only now responding seriously to the storytelling revival as a phenomenon with potentially important implications for the notion of "traditional storytelling" in the United States.[55]

As I noted, John Campbell and Francie Kennelly have both participated in the International Storytelling Festival in London[56]; Belfast too now has a yearly festival.[57] In addition, American storytellers with Irish roots or otherwise (and probably storytellers from elsewhere) are traveling to Ireland to seek out traditional storytellers and their tales in order to gather materials for their own performances back home. There is bound to be some ripple effect as more of the Irish storytellers become aware of the renewed interest in (and market for) traditional tales and the outside venues for their storytelling talents. Given the relatively advanced age of most of the storytellers I interviewed in Ireland and the fact that the tradition has declined almost completely at the local level, one can only speculate on what the possible effects of the storytelling revival might be, how long such changes might take, and whether or not the phenomenon will receive any attention from Irish folklorists. It is worth noting, however, that in the last two decades the number of professional storytellers in the United States (many of whom tell traditional tales) has grown remarkably with very little regard for American folklorists or their preoccupation with "traditionality."

In looking at Ireland today we see a country in transition, and the picture is one of great contrast. Urbanization, modernization, educational opportunity, the tremendous rise in the standard of living, and the development of a consumer economy all militate against the maintenance of the values and traditions that were, and are still, to some degree, a part of Irish rural life. Irish traditional culture is essentially conservative, consensual, and communal; it is not highly individualistic.[58] By the standards of city life it is slow, unhurried, and very personal. As the rural population continues to decrease, the interests and resources of Irish politicians are directed more toward the problems of their constituencies, which are ever increasingly urban: housing, crime, drugs, unemployment—the usual problems of urban life. The longstanding problems of the *Gaeltacht* areas, particularly depopulation and unemployment, remain unsolved. The domains of Irish rural and urban life become increasingly disparate and their better interests more polarized. One can sense in going from Dublin to Carna that one has traveled more than mere miles: one has entered another cultural milieu.

As one might expect when cultural change has occurred so rapidly, some of its effects are less than welcome to many people. Certainly the older people are appreciative of their warmer homes, of the medical care they receive, of the easier life they lead. The farmers appreciate the tractors that keep them dry and let them work in the rain.[59] But many—and not just "the old people"—miss the camaraderie and the more egalitarian, less materialistic quality of life in the past and prefer to live by its standards. They realize that in some respects modern urban culture is international; it is the values and the customs of rural life that represent what is distinctively Irish. The fact that Irish traditional life has been so conservative allows individuals a certain degree of choice, an alternative cultural realm in which to participate. Young and old, given individual propensities, exercise these choices, as we can see in the fact that there is any interest in the storytelling tradition at all; that some Irish people, however few (relative to the problem), attempt to learn the Irish language;[60] that the popularity of traditional music is greater than it has ever been; that there is an influx into many country towns every weekend of young people from Dublin who do not wish to sever completely their connections with country life. The popularity of Eamon Kelly's storytelling attests to the emotional pull of the frame of reference that the persona of "The Shanachie" represents. Everywhere I went in Ireland I met and talked to people who lamented the lack of radio and television programming (both are semi-nationalized) dealing with Irish subjects and utilizing the talents and resources of the people of the countryside. If the public demand for programs of this kind is not great enough, such changes are not likely to occur.[61]

As I have stated, the custom of nightly visiting—the most important context for the telling and learning of traditional narratives—has decreased enormously, resulting in the decline of the tradition and the disappearance of informed audiences for traditional storytelling at the local level. I have no doubt that the interest in traditional narrating in Irish will continue indefinitely. Storytelling, in the broadest sense, will likewise remain. The process of narrating is a universal form of human behavior; indeed, it has been argued that the organization of experience into narrative form is a basic function of human cognition.[62] If the "guardians of the tradition"—Irish folklore scholars—could ultimately develop (or adopt) an ideology that would link storytelling in English to the study of the process of tradition and to the study of cultural history, this, in combination with other contemporary forces, might help to retrieve this aspect of Irish traditional life from the cultural netherworld to which it has been relegated.[63]

Notes to Chapter Three

1. Henry Glassie, *Irish Folktales* (New York: Pantheon Books, 1985), p. 19. In the "Introduction" Glassie discusses in detail the evolution from the literary to the "scientific" treatment of folktales.

2. Douglas Hyde, *Beside the Fire: A Collection of Irish Gaelic Folk Stories* (London: David Nutt, 1890).

3. Ibid., p. x.

4. Ibid., p. xv.

5. Ibid., p. xv.

6. Ibid., p. xvii.

7. The Pale was established through the Statues of Kilkenny, a series of laws the principal aim of which was to strengthen the English presence in Ireland in every possible way. As defined during the reign of Richard II (who succeeded to the British throne in 1377), the Pale ran from Dundalk (in County Louth) to the Boyne, and down the River Barrow to County Waterford. Although frequently broken or discontinued, the Statutes were not finally repealed until 1613. Paul Johnson, *Ireland: A Concise History from the Twelfth Century to the Present Day* (London: Granada, 1981), pp. 24-25. Under the Statutes, English colonists in Ireland were, among many other things, forbidden to speak Irish, to participate in Gaelic sports, to dress in Irish attire, to marry the Irish, to Gaelicize their names, or to submit any legal matters to Irish law. The Irish were forbidden entry to Roman Catholic religious institutions (monasteries, abbeys, or religious orders). Seamus MacCall, *A Little History of Ireland* (Portlaoise, Co. Laois: The Dolmen Press, 1973), p. 17.

8. Patrick K. Ford, "You Just Come to Me and I'll Blind You with Irish," *Folklore and Mythology* 3 (July 1984): 4.

9. Caoimhín Ó Danachair, "The Irish Folklore Commission," *The Folklore and Folk Music Archivist* 1 (Spring 1961): 4.

10. English language narratives are categorized by the terms derived from Irish genres and subgenres, which (with certain notable exceptions) follow the basic conventions of folklore genres. Some examples include *sean-sgéalta*, "folktales" or *Märchen*; *seanchas*, local legends; and *siscéalta*, fairy stories. A comparison of the nomenclature can be seen in the contents of the Irish and English versions of *Seán Ó Conaill's Book*, first published in Irish in 1948. See *Leabhar Sheáin Í Chonaill*, ed. Séamus Ó Duilearga (Baile Átha Cliath: Comhairle Bhéaloideas Éireann, 1948); and *Seán Ó Conaill's Book*, ed. Séamas Ó Duilearga, trans. Máire MacNeill (Baile Átha Cliath: Comhairle Bhéaloideas Éireann, 1981).

11. J. H. Delargy, "The Gaelic Story-Teller. With Some Notes on Gaelic Folk-Tales," *Proceedings of the British Academy* 31 (1945): 180-81.

12. Hyde, p. xli. The "Preface" to *Besdie the Fire* is in English.

13. Patrick K. Ford, "Competence and Competition in Irish Storytelling Tradition," a paper presented at the annual meeting of the Modern Language Association, Houston, Texas, December 1980, p. 3.

14. J. E. Caerwyn Williams, *Y Storïwr Gwyddeleg a'i Chwedlau* (Cardiff: University of Wales Press, 1972), p. 89. A "special" or "archaic" quality of language is common to literary and oral genres in many cultures. In "The 'Pretty Language' of Yellowman," J. Barre Toelken discusses stylistic features, including archaic diction, in the Coyote narratives of the America Navaho. See J. Barre Toelken, "The 'Pretty Language' of Yellowman: Genre, Mode, and Texture in Navaho Coyote Narratives," *Genre* 2 (1969): 211-35.

15. A discussion of the formulaic, descriptive passages associated with storytelling of this kind can be found in Williams [Ford], pp. 105-107. *Folktales of Ireland*, ed. Sean O'Sullivan (Chicago: University of Chicago Press, 1966), pp. 79-117, contains several translations of Gaelic tales that include such runs.

16. Williams [Ford], pp. 90-91.

17. Ford, "Competence and Competition in Irish Storytelling Tradition," p. 4.

18. Donal Moore, Seán Ó Duinnín, and Seán Ó Flannagáin, all narrators of stories in Irish, discussed with me the difficulty of translating some passages of Irish narratives into meaningful English.

19. See Ruth Dudley Edwards, *An Atlas of Irish History* (London: Methuen & Co., 1973; reprint ed., London and New York: Methuen & Co., 1981), p. 244.

20. The *Oireachtas* is sponsored by the Gaelic League, which was founded in 1893. The aim of the Gaelic League is to preserve and encourage the use of the Irish language.

21. Seán Ó Duinnín, Seán McDermot, Éamonn Ó Donnghaile, Seán Ó Flannagáin, and Cáit O'Sullivan—all narrators of stories in Irish—mentioned many additional contexts in which they perform. Seán Ó Duinnín is a traditional musician as well, and he often tells a story of some kind in the settings in which he performs musically. He is occasionally invited to give demonstrations of traditional storytelling to young schoolchildren. Seán McDermot lives in Inveran, Co. Galway. He narrates at local gatherings and storytelling competitions, at *ceilis*, at Irish colleges in the *Gaeltacht* areas, and at informal gatherings of many kinds. Éamonn Ó Donnghaile told me he is always expected to tell a story at wakes he attends; for the musical evenings that are planned in the locality he tells stories in the breaks between performances. He is a widower with six children, and he tells stories for them as well. Éamonn told me that an effort is being made to revive storytelling among the children of the area at the local youth club (in Carna, Co. Galway). Seán Ó Flannagáin has been on the radio on several occasions. Cáit O'Sullivan will tell stories in a pub in Ballyferriter (Co. Kerry) which is receptive to such activities. She has told stories on *Radio na Gaeltachta* and on television, and has been recorded by many people over the last twenty years.

22. It is possible, as well as ironic, that over the course of time Irish may become the language of an educated, urban elite—those actively seeking to learn the language—rather than the vernacular language of the *Gaeltacht* areas.

23. Dell Hymes, "Breakthrough into Performance," in *Folklore: Performance and Communication*, ed. Dan Ben-Amos and Kenneth Goldstein (The Hague: Mouton & Co., 1975), p. 18.

24. Tom Munnelly mentioned that he experienced the same difficulty when listening to Packie's stories.

25. Motifs in "The Quarryman's Son" include F211.1, "Entrance to fairyland through door in knoll"; H1213, "Quest for remarkable bird caused by sight of one of its feathers"; B102.1, "Golden bird,"; H1233.6, "Animals help hero on quest"; B401, "Helpful horse"; B211.3(C), "Speaking horse"; D815.2, "Magic object received from father"; F841.1, "Ship of extraordinary material"; D1011.2, "Magic ear of animal." Stith Thompson, *Motif-Index of Folk-Literature*, rev. ed., 6 vols. (Bloomington, Indiana: Indiana University Press, 1955-58). Motifs numbers succeeded by a "(C)" are to be found in Tom Peete Cross, *Motif-Index of Early Irish Literature* (Indiana University Folklore Series, no. 7. Bloomington, Indiana: Indiana University Press, 1952). Abundant references to printed and archival versions of this tale can be found in Stith Thompson, *The Types of the Folktale: A Classification and Bibliography*, 2d rev. (Helsinki: Folklore Fellows Communications, No. 184, 1961) and Seán Ó Súilleabháin and Reidar Th. Christiansen, *The Types of the Irish Folktale* (Helsinki: Folklore Fellows Communications, No. 188, 1963).

26. "The Mac a hAon Fionn" is a version of Type 369, *The Youth on a Quest for His Lost Father*. "Fin MacCool, Faolan, and the Mountain of Happiness," a version of this story, can be found in Jeremiah Curtin, *Hero-Tales of Ireland* (London: Macmillan & Co., 1894), pp. 484-513. Two stories in O'Sullivan's *Folktales of Ireland* share many of the motifs found in Donal's narrative. "Céatach," pp. 38-56, contains the fight with the giant cat, various hags, the resuscitation of soldiers, the monster's

returning head. "The Coming of Oscar" is essentially a version of the same tale (Type 369), pp. 60-79. Related themes and motifs can also be found in the following narratives: "King Mananaun," in William Larminie's *West Irish Folk-Tales and Romances* (London, n.p., 1893; reprint ed. Freeport, New York: Books for Libraries Press, 1972), pp. 64-84; "Gilla na Grakin and Fin MacCumhal," in Jeremiah Curtin's *Myths and Folk-Lore of Ireland* (London: Macmillan & Co., 1890; reprint ed., New York: Weathervane Books, 1975), pp. 244-269; and "Fin MacCool, Ceadach Og, and the Fish-Hag," in Curtin's *Hero-Tales of Ireland*, pp. 463-483. The motifs include H1381.2.2.1, "Boy twitted with illegitimacy seeks unknown father"; T646, "Illegitimate child taunted by playmates"; F531, "Giant"; B871.10(C), "Giant cat"; H1210, "Quest assigned"; H1219.1*(C), "Quest assigned as payment for gambling loss"; H1248*(C), "Object sought brings about death of assigner of quest"; B871.10*(C), "Giant cat"; D1472.1.8, "Magic table-cloth supplies food and drink"; D615, "Transformation combat"; G263, "Witch enchants or transforms"; D1005, "Magic breath"; G263.5, "Witch revives dead"; G635.1, "Monster's returning head"; B211.9, "Speaking bird"; N2, "Extraordinary stakes at gambling"; Q40, "Kindness rewarded": E155.1, "Slain warriors revive nightly"; E55.3, "Resuscitation by blowing trumpet."

27. John has also performed at the International Storytelling Festival in London.

28. John told me that there was an American comedian whose storytelling style he particularly admired. He could not remember his name, but from his description I think he was referring to George Burns.

29. This is Mr. Campbell's name for this tale. He used a number of other but similar titles when referring to it.

30. "Above and Beyond the End of the Earth" is an amalgam of Types 465B, *Quest for Golden Hair*, and 531, *Ferdinand the True and Ferdinand the False*. A version of this story, "The Red Pony," can be found in William Larminie's *West Irish Folk-Tales and Romances*, pp. 211-18. Henry Glassie's *Irish Folktales* contains two related stories that share many motifs and episodes with Mr. Campbell's. See Glassie, "The Mule" and "The King of Ireland's Son," *Irish Folktales* (New York: Pantheon Books, 1985), pp. 277-285, and corresponding notes (p. 352). The international type index and Ó Súilleabháin and Christiansen's *The Types of the Irish Folktale* also contain references to the above types. Seán Ó Súilleabháin and Reidar Th. Christiansen, *The Types of the Irish Folktale* (Helsinki: Folklore Fellows Communications, No. 188, 1963). Motifs include H1233.6, "Animals help hero on quest"; B401, "Helpful horse"; B211.3(C), "Speaking horse"; S112, "Burning to death"; L160, "Success of the unpromising hero (heroine)"; B181.4(C), "Magic horse travels on sea or land"; C991, "Quest imposed for breaking tabu"; H1241.1, "Hero returning from successful quest sent upon another"; H1248, "Object sought brings about death of assigner of quest"; H1321, "Quest for marvelous water"; H1301.1.2, "Quest for faraway princess"; D2121, "Magic journey"; B181.6(C), "Flight on magic horse"; H75, "Identification by a hair."

31. W. F. H. Nicolaisen, "Concepts of Time and Space in Irish Folktales," in *Celtic Folklore and Christianity*, ed. Patrick K. Ford (Santa Barbara, Calif.: McNally & Loftin, 1983), p. 150. In this essay Nicolaisen discusses the special quality of time and space in Irish folktales and, by extension, in folk narratives generally. Nicholaisen gives some examples, pp. 152-53, of openings of stories which invoke "narrative time."

32. Packie Murrihy and Donal Moore retained formulaic closings to their stories, although not invariably. Packie usually concluded a story with something like "...and if they don't live happy, that we may"; Donal, by saying, "...and that was the story that's in that one," or "that was the story that was in it." (In Donal's case, this is a literal translation into English of the Irish word *ann*, literally "in it," that is, "there" [as in "there were many people there"]). However, most traditional formulaic closings are more elaborate that these, even in English, which suggests to me that both Packie and Donal may have dropped them from their stories because in the more recent contexts in which they have performed, expectations are lowered.

33. At the time that I interviewed him, Francie had only recently begun to think of himself as a storyteller and to narrate in public settings. It is possible that his style might change with further exposure to other storytellers. On the other hand, the general public has so little awareness of traditional storytelling that Francie's style may be an acceptable one in the contexts in which he now narrates.

34. A traditional greeting to workmen in Ireland.

35. This story (Type 1178, *The Devil Outriddled*) also shares a number of motifs and episodes also associated with Type 810, *The Snares of the Evil One*. The international type index contains references to Type 1178, and a large number of references to Type 810 can be found in both the international type index (pp. 274-75) and *The Types of the Irish Folktale*. A much less-developed version of this story, "Friar Brian," can be found in Douglas Hyde's *Legends of Saints and Sinners* (Dublin: The Talbot Press, 1915), pp. 210-13. A substantially different "Friar Brian," but still involving a contract with the devil, appears in *Seán Ó Conaill's Book*, pp. 120-21. Copious references to the latter version appear in the notes to the story (#24), p. 385. Henry Glassie's *Irish Folktales* contains several stories about outwitting the devil, although he ascribes to them a different type number (1187). See Glassie, pp. 116-18, and corresponding notes to the tales (##43 and 44, p. 344). Motifs in "The Gentlemen's Agreement" include N4, "Devil as gambler"; V21, "Confession brings forgiveness of sin"; M210, "Bargain with the devil"; K218.1, "Devil cheated by having priest draw a sacred circle around the intended victim"; D1381.11, "Magic circle protects from devil"; N4.2, "Playing game of chance (or skill) with uncanny being"; G303.3.1.2, "The devil as a well-dressed gentleman"; G303.16, "How the devil's power may be escaped or avoided"; M211, "Man sells soul to the devil"; G303.9.4, "The devil as tempter."

36. As I have noted, a narrator may be both a *seanchaí* and *scéalaí*. Many narrators tell stories in both categories.

37. As Bo Almqvist notes in an article on the Kerry storyteller Micheál Ó Gaothín (son of Peig Sayers), "first rate storytellers *combine pride in the long hero tales and Märchen with a certain...contempt for shorter anecdotes and jokes....*" [my emphasis]. Bo Almqvist, "The Fisherman in Heaven," *Béaloideas* 39-41 (1971-73), p. 19.

38. Jacko McGann died in 1985.

39. Perhaps Junior has a particular liking for this story. However, earlier in our interview I asked him if there was any story he particularly liked to tell, to which he replied no, that he liked them all.

40. A tale in which a mortal's participation in a fairy hurling match works against him can be found in Henry Glassie's *Irish Folktales* ("Fairy Property"), pp. 153-54. Other tales about human involvement in fairy sport appear in the following works: Sean O'Sullivan's *Legends from Ireland* (London: B. T. Batsford, 1977), pp. 73-75; T. Crofton Croker and Sigerson Clifford, *Legends of Kerry* (Tralee, Co. Kerry: The Geraldine Press, 1972), pp. 19-22, and pp. 74-77. A song about a fairy football match appears in D. K. Wilgus, "Irish Traditional Narrative Songs in English: 1800-1916," in *Views of the Irish Peasantry*, ed. Daniel J. Casey and Robert E. Rhodes (Hamden, Conn.: Archon Books 1977), p. 123. Wilgus notes, p. 115, that there are few stories dealing with fairies, ghosts, or Christianity in the Anglo-Irish ballad tradition of this period (1800-1916). Motifs in "The Fairy Football Match" include: D1723, "Magic power from fairy"; F331, "Mortal wins fairies' gratitude by joining in their sport"; F262.3.4, "Fairy music causes sleep"; F267, "Fairies attend games"; F278.2, "Fairies create magic concealing mist"; D813, "Magic object received from fairy"; D1355.3, "Love charm"; F340, "Gifts from fairies."

41. *-ín* here is a Gaelic diminutive suffix (literal meaning, "little") often affixed to English words as well as Irish (*tigín*, "little house," but also "man-ín", "sleep-ín", etc.).

42. A description of a being like "Felix," who also takes up residence with mortals, can be found in Lady Gregory's *Visions and Beliefs in the West of Ireland*, 2 vols. (New York, 1920; reprint ed., Gerrard's Cross, Buckinghamshire: Colin Smythe, 1970), pp. 219-20. Motifs in "Felix" include F62.1, "Bird carries person to upper world"; F601, "Extraordinary companions"; F980, "Extraordinary occurrences concerning animals"; F982, "Animals carry extraordinary burden"; F1021, "Extraordinary flights through air"; B552, "Man carried by bird."

43. "It is generally conceded that the parish of Carna, in West Galway, had more unrecorded folktales in 1935 than did all the rest of western Europe." Seán Ó Súilleabháin, "Introduction" to *Folktales of Ireland*, p. xxxvii.

44. Éamonn's father, Bartley Ó Donnghaile, was a noted storyteller and *seanchaí*. Éamonn told me that it often happened that local *seanchaí* who wanted to ascertain the accuracy of their version of an event would consult with Bartley and other historians until they arrived at as accurate a recounting as possible. Éamonn's comments regarding the unacceptability of any "second version" of a historical event are additionally interesting because of the fact that the medieval *seanchas* material often contains

references to alternative versions of stories, episodes in stories, etiological legends, and the like. (cf., e.g., *Cóir Anmann* ["The Fitness of Names"] and the *Dindshenchas* ["Place-Name Lore"]).

45. According to Éamonn, a "cardinal rule" of *scéalaíocht* was that the narrator had to tell a tale as he heard it (i.e., to maintain the structural integrity of a story). Once again comparing the medieval tradition, in the celebrated colophon at the end of the Book of Leinster version of the *Táin Bó Cuailnge*, future reciters of the tale are charged to tell it as they originally heard it. See Thomas Kinsella, trans., *The Tain* (Dublin: Dolmen Press, 1969), pp. 282-83, n. 253.

46. *Rámscéalaíocht* means the act of storytelling, or "silly talk."

47. This issue came to my attention late in the period I spent talking to narrators in the *Gaeltacht* areas.

48. Donal Moore suggested that I talk to Michael O'Connell, whom he considered to be a well-educated man and knowledgeable about Irish culture, which I did.

49. Cáit O'Sullivan interpreted my questions in terms of the role of women in the storytelling tradition, and replied by saying, "You'd [a woman] be making a tomboy of yourself..." [for narrating the longer stories, particularly hero tales]. Seán merely said that often the *scéalaí* and the *seanchaí* were combined in one storyteller (as did Éamonn). Michael O'Connell used the term *seanchaí* to apply collectively to traditional storytellers, although he acknowledged that, technically, it denoted a "historian." Michael added that he may have been instrumental in perpetuating the more modern usage of this term by painting the sign for one of the rooms in a Reenroe hotel (Ballinskelligs). The room is called "The Seanachie."

50. Mr. Lenihan usually narrates in Irish and had never told these stories in English before.

51. Patrick K. Ford, "Competence and Competition in Irish Storytelling Tradition," p. 5. The idea that different languages represent differing ways of perceiving and expressing "reality" comes, of course, from Whorfian linguistic theory. For an example of Whorf's exposition of his ideas, see Benjamin Lee Whorf, "Science and Linguistics," in *Language, Thought, and Reality: Selected Writings of Benjamin Lee Whorf*, ed. John B. Carroll (Cambridge, Mass.: The Technology Press of Massachusetts Institute of Technology, 1957), pp. 207-219. For an example of these ideas applied to the religious world of the American Navajo see, Barre Toelken, "Seeing with a Native Eye: How Many Sheep Will It Hold?" in *Seeing with a Native Eye: Essays on Native American Religion*, ed. Walter Holden Capps (New York: Harper & Row, 1976), pp. 9-24.

52. Personal conversation with Professor Bo Almqvist, January 27, 1984.

53. For an example of recent work on this subject see, Éilís Ní Dhuibhne, "Dublin Modern Legends: An Intermediate Type List and Examples," *Béaloideas* 51 (1983): 55-70.

54. Richard Handler and Jocelyn Linnekin, "Tradition, Genuine or Spurious," *Journal of American Folklore* 97 (July-September 1984): 273. In this article the authors present a cogent argument for regarding "tradition" as a process of interpretation and ascription rather than as a preexisting entity with well defined boundaries.

55. The American Folklore Society held its first panel on the urban storytelling revival in the United States at its annual meeting in Oakland, California, in October 1990.

56. The British government, in fact, brought John Campbell over to the East Coast of the United States in the fall of 1990 where he performed in a number of venues with traditional singer from Northern Ireland, Len Graham. Personal correspondence, Carmel McGill, Northern Ireland Cultural Exchanges Officer, April 10, 1990.

57. The first storytelling festival was held in Belfast in 1989.

58. The intensely conservative nature of Irish culture, including its oral and literary traditions, has been noted and discussed by many and in multifarious contexts. See, for example, Vivian Mercier, *The Irish Comic Tradition* (Oxford: Oxford University Press, 1962) and Terence Brown, *Ireland: Social and Cultural History, 1922-79* (Glasgow: Fontana, 1981), pp. 13-44, 180-82.

59. Professor Patrick Ford related to me a conversation he had with a man on Inishmore, the largest of the Aran Islands. In reply to Professor Ford's comments about the number of new homes being built on Inishmore (which Professor Ford assumed were built by outsiders), the islander replied that the new houses, which were modern and warm, were built by the islanders for themselves. They sold or rented out the old cottages, which were cold and damp [and "quaint"], to the tourists who come to the islands and who seek this rustic quality.

60. Part of the irony of the situation in Northern Ireland is that it has engendered a tremendous interest in Irish culture and in the language among some of its people. Many who are interested in learning or improving their Irish come into the *Gaeltacht* areas of Donegal for this purpose. Because I thought that it is possible that there is a larger number of people in the North making an active effort to acquire some fluency in Irish than in the Republic of Ireland, and as I had seen no statistics on it, I wrote to Professor Anders Ahlqvist at University College, Galway, on the subject (February 1987). Professor Ahlqvist's response offers some support for my theory. He states, "I do suspect that you are right in implying that those [adults?] who study Irish in the North do so out of a more committed motivation than their equivalents on this side of the border, but I have no means of proving that...statistics are hard to come by and notoriously mendacious in any case." Personal correspondence, March 3, 1987.

61. The Irish television service (*Radio Telefís Éireann*) was inaugurated by the government in 1962. It is subsidized by the government. Although commercials are shown, they do not interrupt programs.

62. The notion that it is a basic function of human cognition to organize experience into narrative form surfaces in the works of scholars in many disciplines and of many theoretical persuasions. For example, in his essay that discusses the resemblance between historiography and literature, Paul Hernadi contends that life itself has "such qualities as epic breadth and tragic depth" that it creates the structure of history. The structure of history, in turn, gives rise to literary genres, including narrative forms. See Paul Hernadi, "The Erotics of Retrospection: Historytelling, Audience Response, and the Strategies of Desire," *New Literary History* 12 (Winter 1981): 243. In "Action and Narration in Psychoanalysis," Roy Schafer examines the role of narrative in the process of psychoanalysis (i.e., the analysand's "recovery"), and suggests that the psychoanalytic process involves the "narrative construction of a second reality" (presumably, a healthier one). This is possible because "language is a set of instructions for narratively constituting events, and the narrative constituting of these events is a uniquely and pervasively human form of action." Roy Schafer, "Action and Narration in Psychoanalysis," *New Literary History* 12 (Autumn 1980): 63, 76.

63. The notion of "cultural history" is emergent in Ireland. As Terence Brown observes, "In Ireland intellectual, cultural and social history are each infant disciplines." Brown, *Ireland: A Social and Cultural History*, p. 10.

Appendix I

Questionnaire

NARRATORS: LIFE HISTORY

1. When and where were you born? Where do you live now?

2. Who are your parents? Where were they from?

    a. What did your parents do?

3. How many brothers and sisters do you have?

    a. What are their ages?
    b. Where did they go and what did they do?

4. Did you get your schooling locally?

    a. How far did you go in school?

5. Were you taught in Irish or English at school?

    a. Did you learn Irish at school?

6. When did you marry and how old were you?

7. When and where was your wife born? What is her name?

    a. What is her age?

8. How many children did you have?

    a. What are their names and ages?

b. Where are they now and what are they doing?

9. What did you do after you left school?

    a. How did you make a living?

10. Have you lived in this area most of your life?

    a. Have you lived or worked in other places?

11. What was your life like as a child?

    a. Was it at all affected by the trouble with Britain or politics in Ireland?
    b. Were you aware of local political activities?
    c. Did the "Black and Tans" ever come through?

STORIES AND STORYTELLING

1. How old were you when you started telling stories?

2. Who did or do you learn your stories from?

3. Under what kinds of circumstances or in what situations did you learn them?

    a. On the same kinds of occasions?
    b. Were there special occasions?

4. In your own family, what were the usual occasions for storytelling?

    a. How many people were usually involved?

5. Did you learn your stories first in Irish or in English?

    a. Were there any stories you learned in Irish and told in English?

6. Did other family members or neighbors tell stories on such occasions?

    a. Were the stories told in Irish or in English?

7. Did you ever tell tales in Irish?

    a. If so, why did you begin to tell them in English?

8. Did you ever learn any stories from books?

    a. Irish or English?

b. Did you tell them just as you read them, or change them?

9. Have you told stories all your life?

   a. Were there ever periods when you stopped? Why?
   b. When did you start again? Why?

10. Did you tell stories to your own children or family?

11. Did anyone over the years come to hear your stories to learn them from you?

    a. When and who?

12. In your own life, how have the audiences for your tales changed?

    a. Who heard them in the past?
    b. Who hears them now? (collectors, children, family, friends, others)

13. How have the situations for storytelling changed since you began telling your tales?

    a. What were they like before?
    b. Where would they be told?

14. Where, when, and to whom do you tell them now?

15. In your own opinion, why would you say these changes have occurred?

    —Reasons (e.g., familial, economic, social, religious, political)

NARRATIVE REPERTOIRE

1. Folktales; hero tales, tales of the fianna

2. Fairy legends and the supernatural (ghosts, "taken away," return of the dead, "in the way," the *bean sidhe*)

3. Religious tales: local priests, wakes, cures (Biddy Early)

4. Saints' legends; local saints

5. Personal experience narratives

6. Local legends: places, famous or infamous people

Consider:

1. Are you telling the same stories that you told in the past?

    a. Do you tell them in the same way?

2. Do you keep learning new tales? From whom?

    a. If you learn a new tale, do you tell it more often than ones you have known longer?

3. Do you ever make deliberate changes in a tale?

    a. Why or why not?
    b. Has this always been true?

4. Does the context (people or place) affect the tale you decide to tell, or how you tell it (content)?

    a. Appropriateness for women, children, others

5. When (what year) did collectors first start coming to see you to record your tales?

    a. Who came first?
    b. Who most recently?

6. How many tales do you think you know?

    a. Have they all been recorded by collectors?

7. Who else likes to hear your stories now?

8. Was your life different before your tales were recorded?

    a. How has it changed things for you?

Appendix II

Ar Cuairt and Related Terms

The following is a list of all the terms I encountered in both English and Irish which refer in some way to the custom of nightly visiting. They are first listed alphabetically according to county and then in subcategories that designate the location, the participants, or the activity denoted by the particular term.

ARMAGH

Participants:
ceili-ers (from *céilidhe*, "to visit"; often spelled "ceili" in English)

Activity:
ceili
ceili-ing

CLARE

Location:
rambling houses
courting houses (presumably from *an chuairt*, literally, "the visit")

Activity:
ragairne (literally, "late hours," "keeping late hours")
an chuairt

CORK

Activity:
scoraíocht (literally, "evening pastime," "social evening")
scoraíocht-ing

DONEGAL

Location:
ceili house

Activity:
céilidhe
ceili-ing
áirneál (Donegal variant of *áirneán*), literally, "night visiting," "sitting up at night"
táimid ag dul ag áirneál (*táimid ag dul*, "we are going"; thus, "we are going *áirneál*")

GALWAY

Location:
teach na cuairt (*teach* is "house"; thus, "house of *an chuairt*")
teach áirneán ("house of *áirneán*")
áirneán house

Activity:
scéalaíocht (literally, "storytelling"; also, "news," "tidings")
(an) cuairtaíocht (the practice of going visiting)
áirneán
ag dhéanamh áirneán ("to be 'at' ["doing"] áirneán")

KERRY

Location:
visiting houses
meeting houses
rambling houses

Activity:
scoraíocht-ing
bothántaíocht (*bothán* is a hut or cabin; thus, the practice of frequenting the neighbors' houses)
teacht ar dhuine mbothán (*teacht*, "going"; *duine*, "person"; therefore, "going to someone's house" ["cabin"])

MAYO

Activity:
cuairtaíocht ("visiting")

Appendix II

OFFALY

Participants:
ceili-ers
ramblers

ROSCOMMON

Location:
rambling house

Participants:
ramblers

Appendix III

Glossary of Gaelic Terms

The glossary contains only those Irish words that occur with some frequency in the text or that have particular importance. Spellings in Modern Irish may vary considerably. (Additional terms not used in the text which refer to the custom of nightly visiting [*ar cuairt*] are listed in Appendix II.)

Áirneán: literally, "night visiting." Refers to the custom of neighborly visits in the countryside.

Ar cuairt: literally, "on a visit." Similar in usage to *áirneán*.

Bothóg (pl., *bothóga*): a small cabin, cottage, or hut.

Ceili: anglicization of *céilidhe*, "to visit." A term used frequently all over Ireland to refer to a gathering for music or other entertainments.

Cóiriú catha: literally, "arrangement for battle." One of several terms referring to the alliterative, descriptive passages found in Irish heroic narrative.

Crua-Ghaedhlig (or *crua-Ghaolainn*): literally, "hard Irish." A type of highly grammatical, archaic diction associated with Irish traditional narrative (in the Irish language only).

Eachtra (pl., *eachtraithe*): literally, "adventure." A category of Irish narrative, often used synonymously with *seanchas*.

Finnscéalta: stories of the Fenian Cycle.

Gaeltacht (pl., *gaeltachtaí*): the areas of Ireland where Irish is still the vernacular language. Sometimes used collectively as *Gaeltacht*.

Appendix III

Oireachtas: a yearly competition of traditional artistic forms, including music and storytelling.

Scéal (pl., *scéalta*; var., *sgéal*, *sgéalta*): literally, "story," "message," "tidings."

Scéalaí: a narrator of long, multi-episodic tales, such as international folktales (Märchen), exempla, and hero tales.

Scéalaíocht: the activity of telling stories.

Scéalta gaisce: literally, "tales of heroism." A category of traditional narrative.

Seanchaí: from *sean*, "old" (variant English spellings: shanachie, sennachie, and others). A narrator of *seanchas*, shorter more realistic stories about ghosts, fairies, and stories of socio-historical import.

Seanchas: one of the two major categories of traditional narrative. Usually refers to family history and genealogical lore, socio-historical material, and realistic tales about encounters with various kinds of supernatural beings.

Sean-sgéalta: literally, "old stories." Refers generally to multi-episodic tales such as international folktales or hero tales.

Síscéalta: literally, "tales of the fairies." A type of legendry and subcategory of *seanchas*.

Spailpín (pl., *spailpíní*): itinerant laborers common in Ireland in the not-too-distant past, and the subject of many stories and songs.

Appendix IV

Selected Tales

PATRICK ("PACKIE") MURRIHY

The Quarryman's Son

There was a man and his wife, and they lived close to a quarry pit here in this country. And the only way he had for living was working every day in, in the quarry, selling the gravel. That was the way he was making his living. Anyhow, this time, 'twas in the wintertime, didn't there a great fall of snow come and, by gar, he couldn't go up in the, in the quarry.

"By God," says he to the wife, Maura, says he, "Yer, whatever about the snow," says he, "but sure we'll be hungry," says he, "if we won't have a handful of gravel to sell," says he. "Give me the shovel," says he.

She get the shovel anyway, and he went to see...[unintelligible]...in his quarry and he felt, pelting the shovels of snow till he cleared a way. And, by God, to his great surprise, didn't he see—didn't a door open, and this man opened the door, and he welcomed him.

"By gar," says he, "I be here a long time," says he, "and how, how well you never come *an chuairt* [the visit] to me?" says he.

"I never knew," says the quarryman, "that the likes of you were there."

"Well, they are," says he. "I'm here," says he. "And you haven't any family?"

"No," says he. "How could I expect to have a family? Sure, poor Maura's an old woman now," says he.

"Ah, never mind about that," says the, the giant inside to him. "Your, your wife will have a, a young son," says he, "in less than twelve months time," says he. And he opened a press [cupboard] anyway, and he gave him a big sum of money. "Well, now," says he, "raise that child," says he, "and when he's seven years," says he, "bring him here to me," says he.

"Yes, sure, I will," says poor Sean. Thought that he'd never have a, any family.

So, by gar, 'tis true for him, hadn't they a young son in less than twelve months' time. He grew up to a nice, strong *garsún* [boy], and they had plenty of money. So

94

he was told by the man in the quarry to educate him. So he did, educated him and all.

And when he was seven, that was the bargain, that he should bring him to the man. So he did. And the mother, she was very lonesome after him. So, they get the man of the quarry a great welcome for him—gave him a grand dinner and all. And, "Well, now," says he, "I won't keep [him] today," says he. "He's too young," says he. "Bring him back," says he, "for seven years more," says he. Gave 'em plenty of money—to feed them all and educate the son. Yerra, sure, she was overjoyed when he came home.

He was fourteen years the second time. So, by gar, he brought him then when he was fourteen, and the mother very lonesome after him. "Well now," says the, the quarryman, "I won't keep him today," says he. "Bring him back," says he, "again," says he, "for seven years more, and he'll be twenty-one then," says he, "and he'll be well able to do for himself then," says he.

So he did. Brought him back when he was twenty-one years. And he brought him first when she was seven, then fourteen, and when she was twenty-one then. He was a young man.

"Well now," says he, "I've a lot of money," says he, "lost supporting that boy," says he, "and yourself and your wife," says he. "So," he says, "I'll keep him anymore now, myself," says he, "and, he'll be a rich man," says he. "He'll never be short of anything," says he.

So, by gar, the father, of course, he was very lonesome after him. And when he was comin' home without him, poor Maura—she was an old woman—and she would, didn't she die of grief when he hadn't the son coming back with him.

Very well. He brought in the son, anyhow, and educated him. And, by gar, he got a job for him. And the job was, with this big man, a gentleman, eight or nine clerks with him. And, when the quarryman, when he was passing with him anyhow, he gave him a pen. "Well now," says he, "keep that pen," says he, "and, any letter or anything, anything you have to write," says he, "place the pen in, in, in the paper," says he, "and 'twill write whatever you want," says he.

So, by gar, he did. He got the job with the other nine clerks with this gentleman. And, by gar, he give a prize to the first done, and the best written. So, the quarryman's son got the prize.

By damned, that went on for a while, anyhow, and prior to that, when he was parting from, from his foster father, "Well, now," says he, "you'll travel through this country now," says he, "and it's fine country," says he. And he gave him a bridle. "Go down to that field below," says he, "where there are grand horses there," says he, "and shake the bridle," says he, "bring him here to me," says he.

He did. He went down to the big field where the horses were, and he shook the bridle. Sure, if he did, whatever, the horses, they ran here and there. And he was coming back again, along an avenue that looked into the house, and didn't he see a little pony there.

"Sure, maybe," says he, "you'll stick your head in the, in the bridle." He shook the bridle, and as soon as he did, didn't the little pony stuck his head into the bridle. Yerra, he brought her home then and fed her and took great care of him.

By gar, this was going on—going on for a long time, and the rest of the clerks, they had a meeting, a meeting between themselves.

"Yerra," says the..., "he'll be always very fond of the pony. When he'd be at his work he'd go out to the stable and feed him, give him a drink and all to that."

"Ah, by gar," says the..., "aren't we the good scholars?" says the....They said they were.

"And how is it," says the..., "that that man," says he, "the one who was to come up to him," says he, "he's such a scholar?" says he. "And I don't know what's ...[unintelligible]...Maybe 'tis in the pen it is," says he.

So, one of them came in one day, in a hurry, and says, and says the pony was sick outside in the stable. Didn't he run away out, and left the pen in the, in the ink bottle. Yerra, as soon as he went, sure they took the pen, placed it in the, in the paper. Yerra, sure, it wrote away whatever, whatever they'd like.

"Ah," says the man, the boss, says he, "there must be something in that pen," says he. He looked at it. 'Twas a grand pen. "That pen," says he, "belongs to a bird," says he, "they call the 'Golden *Féinics*'" [phoenix].

So now says the boss to him, says he, "Go out," says he, "now and bring that bird here."

"By gar, I don't know," says he.

"Well go," says he.

And he went back to his so-called father, and he told him the story. Well, the father and mother there anyway, they gave him his blessing anyway, and the father said to him, "You'll have to go on horseback today," says he. So they put a grand saddle on the pony, and off he went.

He was travelin' away, anyhow, on his journey, didn't he see a big giant, and he tied up to a big tree. And a lot of meat and eatables was left in, in, in the plate under the tree.

"Oh God," says he, "I'm dying," says he. "I'm dying with the hunger," says he. "Can you do anything for me?" he says, to the quarryman's son.

"Come off," says the, says the pony to him, "and you'll get a, a knife," says she, "here in my ears," says she. "And cut—cut the rope," says she, "and let him down."

He did. Yerra, sure he ate an awful feed. He said he was there for two or three days. "And they plagued me," says he. "Sure, they put these eatables in the—and sure I couldn't, I, I couldn't release myself," says he. "But remember me," says he. "I have two other brothers," says he, "stronger men than what I am," says he. "And if ever you're in any trouble," says he, "come to me, and I'll, I'll, I'll do all I can for you." He went up on the pony. Off he went again.

By God, when he was traveling on, anyhow, didn't he see a hawk above in a tree and he, and he killing, killing the young eagles, and throwing 'em down. "Come off," says the pony to him, "and save the young eagles," says he. "They might be help to you." So, he did. And he saved the young eagles.

"Now," says the mother eagle, says she, "that's the man," says she, "that saved your life," says she. "And remember me," says she to the quarryman's son. "If you're ever, ever in any trouble," says she, "come to me," says she, "and we'll do all we could for you."

Off he went again, anyhow, and what was she—she was traveling near a river, I believe. And he saw a water dog in the river, and another big water dog was coming to eat him. "Come off," says he. "That stick—cane you have in your hand," says he, "kill one of them other eagles," says he, "and save the young eagles." Or the young, the young—they were hounds, yes. Water dogs they were. And he did.

He went on, anyhow, in search of the, in search of the pen. So, by damned, he was travelin' away for it anyhow, and begar, he was told that that Golden *Féinics* was in another island. And, "You're better to go there," says, says, says the, says the pony to him, "and you'll get the bird there," says she, "standing in a, in a, in a perch," says she, "near the house," says she. [CH: In a perch, Packie?] Yes, the bird was standing..."And bring her here to me," says he.

But before they started, anyhow, he got an account that the bird was in such a country. So she told him, anyhow, to pull a feather out of a wing—clean off the feather and dip it in the water. "And that'll make a boat for you," said she.

So he did. And he arrived in the island anyhow. And he met a man and he told him where he was going. "Well now," says he, "that bird," says he..."This country you're in now, said he, "they've slept," says he, "for seven years," says he, "and in seven years they awoke," says he, "so take off your boot," says he, "and, in order that they won't feel you," says he.

And he did. And didn't he get the cage, and the bird, and brought it back. Went into the, into the boat again. And he came back. He came back to the man that sent him first, do you see?

Well, he had three sons. Yerra, sure, didn't they fall...Oh, he had the bird anyhow, and the bird was a fine singer. But when they brought her to this place, anyhow, wasn't he putting only his head under his wing, and there was no, no singing. [CH: He wouldn't sing a note.] No singing.

"By gar," says the boss to him, says he, "you're better to go again," says he, "and bring, and bring, bring that bird here," says he.

By gar, didn't he think of himself then and went to, and he told the story to the eagle. The eagle called the young eagles. "Go now," says the..., "and bring back...."

"She can't sing," says he, says one of the...[unintelligible]..., "when she hasn't her, her mate with her."

"Go now," says he, "and bring her here to me," says he.

"Ah well, how will I go?" says he.

"Well, you must go," says he, "or, or if you don't," says he, "you'll be killed."

He told the pony. He told the pony anyhow. "Come on," says the pony. "We'll go now to...Bring that lady here," says he, "that owns that bird," says he, "and that bird'll sing."

So he had three sons, and he brought back the bird, the Golden *Féinics*. And gar, when he did, standing before he had his only his head under his wing.

"Ah," says one of them, "that's some enchantment." "She can't sing," says she, "when she hasn't her, her mate here with her." Faith, they told the quarryman's son to go and to bring it here.

So he had to go off again. And he, he went into the boat anyway, and, the lady was sleeping anyhow, and didn't he bring his hands, hands around her. He brought everything into the boat, and he told the boat to bring me, to bring me to Ireland. So the boat came of his own accord and brought him to the Ireland. So...And the bird didn't sing.

"Ah," says one of them," says he, "she can't sing," says he, "when her, her, her mate isn't here. We'd better to go," says he, "to the quarryman's son, and go again and, bring her, and bring her here." Which he did.

He went this time anyway by the boat—by boat, and he came to the island. And didn't he put his hands around her and brought her in, and put her into the boat. And they landed in Ireland.

"Well," says she, "I came here," says she, "but I'm very wealthy, and when I was coming in the boat, my wealth is no good to me," says she. "I was frightened," says she, "when this man," says she, "took me by surprise, and I threw all the keys," says she, "into the western ocean. But I can't marry your son," says she, "till, till he gets..."

[Family members interrupt here to offer tea, so the tape recorder is turned off. Packie resumes his storytelling about ten minutes later, after he has reviewed the end of what was previously recorded.]

Well, when he brought her back anyhow, "I can't marry your son," says she, "because I'm very wealthy, and all my keys are gone. They're thrown into the—I was very frightened," said she, "and I threw, threw 'em into the western ocean," says she. "And I can't marry your son," says she, "till I get them keys."

So, he came to the quarryman's son. "You better go again," says he, "and get them keys for me," says he.

He told the pony 'bout it. "Come on now," says the pony. "We'll go to see—to the hound," says he, "and—or to the water dog. And maybe send out the water dog," says she, "to search for them keys."

And so, he did, and she told the water dog about it. And she put two of her, she put two of her pups to search for the, for the keys. And they came back without them. All to the fact that their, their toes were all cut from going through the, the rocks. And, they said to the mother—mother water dog, "Ah," says she, "you're no good," says she. "I'm better to go myself," says she.

The water dog went off herself—their mother—and she was searching and searching, went through rocks and all, and she got the keys and put them in her mouth and brought 'em back. "Now," said she to the quarryman's son, "isn't that the keys for you now?"

He went back to the boss then, and he gave him, he gave him the keys. "Well now," he told the son—the eldest son that was going to be marrying, "Well," says he, "I can't sing," says she, "till..." What'll I see, was that it? Wait'll I see. The water dog got the keys, and the eagle got the, got the....[CH: Well, you have a lot of distractions, Packie, so...] Well, yes. "Well go again," says...[unintelligible]..."and, and bring back the, the girl—the mate."

So as far as that she brought her back. And she couldn't sing till she have all, all the, the wild animals that were in front of her, her hob at home, and the bird would be up there, and the bird would sing when it sees them things. So, he told the pony about it. "Come on, now," says he. "We'll go to that strong man," says she, "that saved his life."

So she—they came to him and he told her. Well, he called his other two brothers. "Come on," says he, to the other two brothers, says he, "and we'll go to the west of it." And they did. And they started blowing and blowing till they put it right in front of the, of the palace, and they settled now.

"Haven't we that done now for you and all?"

"Well," says she, "I can't, I can't sing," says she, "now," says she. "I want to marry your son," says she, "but, where I live," says she, "off to the west, there is a—three wells there," says she, "and the Water of Life, and the Water of Death, and the Water of Beauty is in, is in, in them three wells. So, I can't marry your son," says she, "till I get that water."

So, he had to go off again. And he told the eagle about it. The eagle told, the two birds, anyhow—or three of them, to go and get 'em, and bring back the water. And they put a cord around their neck and the bottle. They bring for each of 'em. One of them bring the Water of Life, and the other Death, and the Water of Beauty. So, by God, didn't they bring 'em.

So, they were preparing for the wedding when she was to be getting married to the eldest son. Well, they'd a great wedding anyhow, and she'd the three bottles. She told the little fella, anyhow, to wash his face in, in that water, which he did. And she put a drop of, of water, out of the bottle, and that was the Water of Death. He washed his face with it and, as soon as he did, he fell dead. Sure, rolled up the little bird that was inside in the room and threw him in under it. And she called the other fella, and she did the same thing to him.

She called in the quarryman's son then. "You're," says she, "the best that earned me," says she. "Wash your face now," says she, "in the Water of Beauty." And he did. "Wash your face now," says she. She threw out a drop of water out of the Water of Life. And, he washed himself in that. "Well, now," says she, "'tis you I'll marry now," says she. "'Tis you that have made way earned."

So that's—they got married and lived happy, and if they didn't that we may. That's the story now.

DONAL MOORE

The Mac a hAon Fionn

There was a great story about the Fianna. Ah, did you ever hear from—Did you ever hear in headline about Fionn MacCumhail? Fionn MacCumhail was the greatest giant that was in Ireland. When Fionn MacCumhail was gianting here in Ireland he had fourteen giants with him, but, uh, they were apprentices. He had a big—He had a big castle in Stake [Staigue] Fort—That's in Caherdaniel. So, he used to keep a great sword, do you see? They all had their—There was a big shed, and it was packed with swords, do you see? They—they were made by, by the armory smiths around, do you see?

But, uh, this day, anyway, there was a big fight to be in Banna Strand, in Dingle. And didn't the sword, when it was hit by the other sword by a, a, a giant from Tuosist, it broke a sword. "Oh, we'll have another go tomorrow," he says.

He—he came tomorrow. He tried every sword he had and, uh, he picked the best, and that got broke again. So, he got beaten there, and he went to a smith—the best smith in Ireland—to make a good sword for him.

So, the smith asked him, "My—my time," he says, "to make a right sword'd be a long time."

"I didn't mind," he said, "if it was twelve months."

"That's just what it would take," he said, to make this—twelve months."

So, this smith, he had two daughters. They were two fine girls. And, "You have to bring me," he says, "a half ton of steel," he says, "and two tons of coal," he says, "to make this sword," he says, "to make it proper."

"I will do that," he said. He did. And he was making the sword. Anyway, as, on the day, it exactly took twelve months to finish it. He finished the sword, and he paid the smith. He took out his wallet and he paid the smith.

"Well, now," says the smith to him, "there is—there is going to be a stay now" [?], he says.

"What is that?" he said.

"Ah, my eldest daughter is pregnant after you. And," he says, "you'll—I'd like to have you wait," he says, "—'tis only two months until the baby's born—to have you give us the name and to have you be there."

"I haven't that much time," he says, "but I'll give you the name, and if it is a son, call him the Mac a hAon Fionn, and if it is a daughter, you can call her any name you like." It were a son, and they baptized him the Mac a hAon Fionn.

So, that was all right. They reared him, and he was going to school. They sent him to school when he was six years. And, the Lord save us, 'twas what was happening in that local school, he was half-killing all the, all the lads that were in the, in the playground, until the master started to control him. So, he took control, you know. He was—He was agreeable. They didn't go near him, like. They were scared of him.

Appendix IV

So, he came home, anyway, after this evening, and he was after being a year and a half in school, and he eight years and a half. And he told his mother that one of the young fellas called him a bastard. "What is the meaning," he says, "of calling me a bastard?"

"Oh, don't mind what young fellows say," she says. "That's always happening."

"Well," he says, "there's one thing here," he said, "that's, mother," he says, "it's no father," he says. "I have a shotgun," he said.

"You have?" she says. "Where did you get it?"

"I got it from a local man," he says, "in order to save my life. And he told me that he was a cousin of yours."

"Oh, he would have it," she said.

"Well, now," he said, "if you don't tell me who my father is, 'tis loaded now," he said. "You'll get the contents of it."

"I will," she said. "You're a son," she said, "of Fionn MacCumhail."

"Fionn MacCumhail?" he says. "Where does he live?"

"He lives," she says, "in the Caherdaniel side in a place called Gort na Chrú [Goirtín a' Chrú], where there is a big castle."

"Make a load for me," he says, "that'll keep me going on the road."

She made as much as she could of sandwiches for him, and he struck out for the road. And he never drew rein until he went to Gort na Chrú. And he knocked at the door—He was small, of course. He was small, of course, he weren't fully grown up but, of course, he was a big man, but he was classified small to be a giant. So he knocked at the door and the maid came out, and he asked her was Fionn MacCumhail in.

"Fionn MacCumhail," she says, "isn't in the position that he'd be seeing or speaking to the like of you at all."

"Well, look here to me," he says. "I'll break that door," he says, "if you don't go in to tell him come out."

"Oh," she says, "I'll go in and I'll tell him to get the police [?] for you."

"Tell him so."

He came out, and Fionn MacCumhail asked him where did he come from. He told him. "Oh yes," he says, "you're my son."

He took him in and the giants—There was a big table and they were eating at this big table, and there was one man, one giant there, he wanted to mock him. He was, uh, Jeremiah Donohue. So, when they'd eat the meat off the bone, you see, they'd leave it aside into a big tray. And what did this Donohue do, but he catched the bone—this bone, there was some scraping on it—and he gave it down to young Fionn, thinking, you see, that it'd run him off—that he couldn't knock much out of it. He ground every bit of it with his teeth. So, that was all right.

Didn't it happen that night that he was put to bed with him, in this big bed. And didn't Donohue, this giant, give the night playing at him. "Well," he says, "if you aren't going to behave yourself," he says to Donohue, he says, "I'll put the nine tines [prongs] in you," he said, "that could never ripped, and I'll hang you out the window."

Donohue only laughed at him. He still played at him. Mac a hAon Fionn jumped out of the bed, and he got this half-twisted cotton rope that was in his pocket. He tied him up and he hung from by the window. And he had [heard?] every roar, and

Fionn left the bed—he knew there was something wrong—and Fionn pulled him in. I tell you, O'Donohue was, was 'fraid, was 'fraid well before him from that out.

So, then in the morning all the giants they were going out hunting with those big razors. Hunting and shooting. So, he said, uh, they were going hunting and shooting, and he, he told her—Oh, Fionn told him that they were going hunting.

"Oh, I will go, too," he says.

"Oh, God, no," he said. "You're too small," he said. "But when you'll get stronger, you'll go. You can stay there," he says, "and you can help the cook," he said, "the rest of the day," he says, "and we'll be back in the evening."

So, faith, when they wanted water and she told him to bring above a pail of water. So, she gave him this bucket. "Oh, my God," he says, "that's too small," he said. There was a big churn there. "That'd be more like it," he said.

"Oh, sure," she said, "you couldn't carry that."

"Oh, yes," says she, "and I will."

He took it down to this big well and brought it full. No trouble to him—forty gallons of water, between his two hands.

So, do you know, but she got jealous of him, she over-thought that, that he was a son of Fionn's. So, by God, anyway, she says, "We'll have a game of cards."

"Fair enough," he says. "I can card-play. What'll we play?"

"We'll play five games," she says. "For which of us—If I, if I win," she says, "I'm going to put on you," she says, "of the request, that you'll have to get the top of the two ears that was taken off a king that was here in Ireland long 'go."

"Fair enough," he said.

They played the second five games, and he won it. He asked—she asked him, "What was the request?"

"Well, I'm putting you on with a hard request," he said. "Where there'd be," he says, "two men," he says, "beating, beating corn," he says, "with a mill—with a millstone, and you to be placed," he says, "behind a standing knitting needle that there is a, there'll be an eye in the end of it, and if when I, until I'll, until I'll find the two ears," he says, "that was taken off the king in Ireland," he says. "That'll be your feeding," he says, "what'll go through the crow of the needle," he says, "until I come back."

Fair enough. 'Twas a law made. And Fionn, old Fionn came, anyhow. They came from the hunting, and he told the father that such a thing—what he, what he had won and what she had won. "And where am I going to get," he says, "those two ears that were taken off of the king in Ireland?"

"I wouldn't be sure of 'em," he said, "but I think they're in County Limerick somewhere."

Ah, "I want a good sword going now," he said.

"You would," said the father, "and, and, and a good loan, a good bit of grub."

"I'd want to carry a lot of grub," he says.

"Oh, no," he says. "I have gifted grub here," he says. "I've a little tablecloth inside there," he said, "and any kind of food you'll ask for," he said, "it'll come on it."

"Fair enough," he said.

"Come on out now," he says, "to the store," he says, "until I'll select a, a sword for you. You can test 'em now yourself," he said, "until you get the best one."

Appendix IV

He caught one, and he shook it, an he made two halves of it. He put twenty-seven of 'em off of him, and he was making two halves of 'em.

"Hold on now," says old Fionn, "I have a special one. And this is your grandfather made it," he said, "and he gave twelve months making it."

He caught it, and he shook it. He made the blade as white as a shilling. He shook it secondly, and he made it as, as pure as ivory. He shook it the third time, and 'twas still the same. "This will work," he said.

Off he went, and he kept traveling. And he went to a farmer's house that night, and he asked the farmer would he give him lodging. He said he would. I wa—The farmer asked him, "There's potatoes boiled there," he says, "and meat."

"No," he says, "I have my own loan," he says. He took out this tablecloth, and he spread it on the table.

"What kind of food would you like?" he says to the farmer.

"I have to be satisfied with what food I have," he says. "I can't afford any special foods."

"I'll give you any food you like," he said. He spread the tablecloth, and he asked for anything and everything, and all things came from the table. And the farmer put down a great feed, himself and his wife.

So, the morning came, and he asked him in the morning would he have any idea who was the, who were the people that took the two ears off of the king here in Ireland long 'go. "Ah, they are there, all right," he said. "But the man that did that," he said, "he comes to a farmer in County Limerick," he says, "in every three years. And the rent that's on him in that farm," he said, "—he's a big rancher—that he'll have to keep him eating in one table for seven years without leaving it."

"I'll make an off [?]," he says. He made an off. And, uh, he asked the farmer would he lea—would he give him lodge tonight.

"I will," he says. "I won't be begging you," he says. "I have my own food."

So they got speaking, anyway, and near the fire, and he asked the farmer what was his living here.

"I'm a big rancher," he says.

"Oh, you're doing great, so," he said.

"I am not," he said. "There's a big rent on me," he said.

"And what is the rent?"

"Oh, there is this big, rich man," he says. "He is a big, a big businessman. And he comes by—he comes to me," he says, "in every three years," he says, "and I'll have to feed him in one table," he says, "for seven years."

"That's very expensive, anyway," he says.

"Otherwise," says the farmer, he says, "I'd have to go out the door," he says.

"Well, now," he says, "I'm spreading this cloth on the table," he says, "and there isn't any food," he says, "that was ever made, but will come on it that you'll care about."

"By gar," he says, "you're a wonderful man."

"Send for him now, tomorrow."

"I don't care to be sending for him because," he says, "he isn't due to come for another year."

"Send him—for him tomorrow," he says, "and it won't put me—it won't cost me nothing," he says.

"By gar," he says, "it's a great story," he said. He sent for him.

So, "What time is he coming tomorrow?" says the *spailpín* [itinerant laborer].

"He'll be coming," he says, "about twelve o'clock."

"How is it," he says, "that that man," he says, "have such an appetite and such a griping desire?"

"Oh, he's a savage man," he said.

"Does he ever do anything bad out of the way," he said, "in this part of the country?"

"Oh, he took the two ears of the king was here long 'go."

"Are you sure he have 'em?"

"I've seen 'em by him," he says.

So, "By God," he says, "that's what I'm out for."

He came anyway, about twelve o'clock, and he sat at the table. He had everything and anything put—called from the table for him that he never got below from the farmer.

"You have a grand table," he said.

"Oh, I am—I have," he says.

"Is that a little Irish fellow there," he says, "sitting in the hearth?"

"Oh, yes, it is," he said.

"God," he said, "'tis long 'go," he says, "I took the top of the two ears off a king," he says, "in Ireland," he says. "And look, Paddy," he says to the farmer, "they're as fresh as ever."

The farmer looked at him. "I never seen 'em," says the farmer.

"God," says Mac a hAon Fionn, "I'd love to see 'em." Do you see?

"Yerra, what do you want seeing 'em, you *créatur*?" he says.

"Well, I'd like to see 'em."

"Well, I suppose," says the farmer, "we—Do you mind that we have a look at 'em?"

He gave 'em to them, and the Mac a hAon put 'em down in a little pocket and walked out the door. And, if he did, faith, this big a lump of a man went out after him. To kill him. He pulled the sword from under his coat, and he blew the head off of him.

So, the robin that was in the tree in the haggard, the robin spoke. "That head," says he, "'ll go back on the body again," he says, "if you can't hit the head."

My God, he was aiming at the head, and he couldn't make it.

"Call," he says, "the wild duck," he says, "that's in the slough. Call the snipe that's in the dyke. Call the duck that's in the lake."

He did, and they were all coming. And the duck that was in the lake came, and the deer—the duck threw her knife from her. The robin told him, "If you don't hit his head with the egg," he says, "he'll be alive as good as he ever was."

He hit him in the head—He hit the head and it coming down with the egg. Body and all fell dead.

"By gar," said the farmer, "but you have good done for me," he said, "and I hope," he says, "I'll try to do good for you."

"So, I must be going home now," he says. "My request is won."

So he was—He shook hands [?] to him and he made—he left goodbye to him. And on his way home in the, Limerick it was getting late in the night, and he said it'd be

Appendix IV

too late to go for Kerry. He asked this man, anyway. He was a big ta—he was a big—No, it was a girl that was inside before him. A big, tall, girl, a very tall girl. And he asked her could he get lodge for the night. She said he would. So, she told him that she—Would he take a meal? "Oh, I have the meal myself," he said. He spread it on the table, and everything came on it; and he told her to sit down to it. "This isn't going to put me back anything," he says.

So, that was well and good and about two o'clock her—this big, tall boy came in. "Glory be to God," he says to the boy, "isn't it late you're out? Are you a member of the house?"

"I am," he said.

"And why are you out so late?" he says.

"I'll tell you then," he says. "I have an orchard," he says, "and 'tis my living. And every time," he says, "every night," he says, "that orchard," he says, "is packed with soldiers," he says. "And I do have, since the dark come," he says, "and 'tis two o'clock, with a sword," he says, "trying to kill 'em. And when I'll go back again in the morning," he says, "they're all alive."

"I'll go with you tomorrow night," he said, "and I won't be long killing 'em," he says. "They might kill you," he says.

"Don't go at all," says the sister, "they might kill you."

"They won't kill me at all," he said.

He went with him the following night. And he had the sword, and he'd have forty heads taken on—off, while the, while the owner of the orchard'd have one. They had it all cleaned up for seven o'clock.

So, "By God," he said, "you're a great man."

"Here, now," says the boy, he says, "we'll go home."

"I won't go home at all," he says. "There is something causing this," he says. "There is something behind this," he says, "that those are coming to life."

"Look," he says, "if they wake up," he says, "—and they will—," he says, "they'll kill you."

"They won't kill me at all," he says, "because I'll down 'em," he says, "as fast as they'll rise."

The boy went away, and he couldn't convince him to go with him.

He sat in near the wall. Mac a hAon sat in near the wall. The next thing was, when the dark came, up jumps two soldiers, and he threw the head off 'em. There was a cease, and he see an old hag coming out from under a hawthorne tree. She took a flute out of her pocket, and she put it into a soldier's ear, and up he jumps, and soldiers from soldier until there was five of them standing. He blew the head of 'em. Down he goes to her. She was a queer one, queer-ín. She fought him. She fought him until he had her nearly killed. He had the best got of her. The blows were taking no effect of her, but still he killed her, and out come this big, black cat, and jumped at his throat, and sucked every drop of blood out of his body.

The boy came in the morning, and there was no soldier standing. And he was looking for the Mac a hAon Fionn. The Mac a hAon Fionn, he choked the cat as well as the cat drawing his blood. The two of them now—the cat was in his throat and the Mac a hAon Fionn had his hand in his throat as well. The two of 'em—the cat was as long as the Mac a hAon, and he got the fright of his life when he see 'em both dead. And he had the flute in his pocket.

He went home, and he told the sister such a thing. She came with him. She was very upset. And whatever way the sister—Man, she was so clever—she see the flute in his pocket, and she took it out.

"What's the meaning of this?" she says, he says to the brother. "It must be this that was doing the damage."

"I wonder," says the brother, "if it was put in his mouth."

"There's no good in putting the mouthpiece in his mouth," she says. "Put the end and—and blow into it."

They blew into it, and he sat there in his body [?].

"Well, now," he says, "I'll be as good as I was any day of my life," he said, "but the cat have all my blood sucked. And you skin the cat," he said, "as careful as anything you ever did," he said. "If there's a hair's breadth of a, of, of a strake [?]," he says, "the blood'll be useless."

"I'm a butcher," says the boy.

"Put on good edge," he says. "I won't live," he says, "without getting my blood back."

Well, he did. Skinned the cat careful, if a cat was ever, if an animal was ever skinned careful. And he told him to stick the cat in the heart. "Two spoons of it'll do me," he said. They pulled four spoons of the blood out of him. And he drank it, and he jumped up as good as he was any day of his life.

So, they went home, and they had a dinner, and a dinner off of his tablecloth. They wanted him to stay with 'em for the rest of their life.

"Now," he says, "for the sake of the soldiers," he says, "we'll plough for you (?)."

"Well, you'll never again," he says, "see a soldier," he says, "alive in that orchard. She was a running evil," he says, "was that old lady," he said. "And she's the only one ever that got the best of me, but I, today, have got the best of her. I must be off now," he says. "There is a request."

He went off, and he traveled until he came to Gort na Chrú, and there she was on the spike before him. He took the two ears of the king that was taken away—off the king that was taken here, off of the king that was taken here in Ireland long 'go. He shook the two ears at him, and she fell dead—with the fright. And he became the greatest giant that was ever in Ireland since then. That's the story.

JOHN CAMPBELL

Above and Beyond the End of the Earth

There was a king in Ireland, and he had three sons. And one of them was a devil-may-care fella, and he went away. And he went to France. And he gadded about in France, uh, and spent all his money. And, uh, eventually, he come back home. And when he come back home, the very day he arrived back home, his father was after being buried.

And the other two sons, when he went into the castle, the other two sons was in the countin' room, dividin' the money. And the minute they saw him, they said, "Where are you going?"

He says, "I'm back home."

"You know father's dead?"

"No, I didn't know that. What are yous doing with the money?"

"We're dividin' it. He left it all between us."

"Did you not leave any for me?"

"No. All he left you is the low meadow—the low, long meadow—down by the river." You see.

So, he was very—he was very disappointed. And, uh, after a day or two, he said to himself, "Well, I better go down and see this land that I got in the low, long meadow down by the river."

And down he went, and when he looked into the meadow, there was three horses in the meadow. And, one of them had a little foal. But the foal was only about the size of a rabbit—a wee, delicate, puny foal. So, he says to himself, "Lord, three fine horses there, and that foal with the spindly legs running after it and..." You know. "I think I'll drown that foal in the river. Going to—not going to waste grass an, an, and a good mare on, that animal."

So he went out and he caught the foal, and he was draggin' the foal down to put it into the river. And when he got to the brow of the river, the foal spoke to him. And he says, "Ah, don't drown me. Give me one chance," he says. "Maybe," he says, "when I get runnin' about and gets the good flush of grass," he says, "I might grow into a big fine colt."

So, he looked at him, and he says, "Well, you're entitled to one chance." And he let him go.

And he went away to France for another twelve months. And after the twelve months he come back again, and when he went down to the low, long meadow beside the, the river, the foal was still there and it didn't grow any bigger. And he was mad. And he crossed into the field, and he caught the wee foal, and he was taking it down to drowned it. And when the wee foal got down to the other river, he says, "I just want one request. There's a saddle," he says, "under the bushes, and will you just take it over and put it on me back, so as I'll have to say when I go in the world—into the world beyond, that there was harness on me back."

So, the man went over. And when he went over there, there was a saddle and bridle and everything where the wee foal told him it was. And he took it over, and he said, "I'll not put it on your back. It'll break...."

"No," he says, "put it on my back." So, he put it on his back.

He says, "Tighten the girt!" And, he tightened the girt.

And when he tightened the girt on the sa, on the saddle, the foal grew into a great big, big horse. Lovely big, black horse.

"Now," he says, "get up on my back," he says, "and I'll, and I'll give you a ride before you drowned me." And he went round the meadow like the wind.

And, uh, the man was all enchanted. "Well," he says, "ah, I'll not the devil to drowned," he says, "I'll do on you," he says. "I'll tell you what. I'm sorry," he says, "but I've to go 'way to France. You stay where—I'll leave the saddle on you," he says, "till I come back."

He says, "Sure, what's taking you to France? I'll take you to France," he says. "You sit where you are."

"Oh," he says, "you couldn't...."

"Oh," he says, "I could take you to France. You just sit where you are, and I'll take you to France."

So he galloped along like the wind. And he galloped along the sea. And he's gallopin' on, and he come to a place where there was a wee, low bridge—humpy-back bridge. And the horse turned 'round, and he says to him, "Now, when I—when we cross this bridge," he says, "don't you speak anymore," he says, "till I land you in France, because if you do," he says, "something'll happen."

So on they galloped along the sea, and it come on dark. And out in the sea, the king's son in the saddle, he saw this thing shinin'. And it grew, and it grew, and it grew, and it grew into a big light. He thought the sea was on fire. And he says to himself, "I wonder what that be." Out loud, like that.

And just with that the horse says, "Damn you for opening your mouth!" he says. "I'll have to swim out there now."

And he swam out. And when he got away out to where this light was, it started to get smaller and smaller until it was just like a silver thread. But it was shinin' in the water. The horse says, "I'm going to swim round in a circle now," he says, "and you put out your hand and catch that," he says. "And the minute you catch it," he says, "put it into your inside pocket."

So, he galloped 'round, and he put out his hand and he caught it, and he put it into his inside pocket. He says, "For that's a hair out of the head of the Queen of Sleepy Island." So, he put it in his pocket, and he thought nothing of it.

And the next thing, they landed in France. And they went up to the King of France, and up he went, and a servant come and took the horse, and they put the horse into a stable. And, he got down, do you see, and shook his clothes. Shook his coat and put it on him again to look a bit respectable goin' in to the King of France.

And when they went in, they were sittin' talkin', and they sat by the window. And all of a sudden the King of France says, "My stables are on fire!" The whole place was lit up.

And they ran out. And when they went down, the hair had fell out of his pocket, and 'twas lyin' on the stable and it had the whole stable lit up. So, he put down his hand to catch it, to lift it to put it in his pocket, and the King says, "Show me that!"

Appendix IV

And the king says, "That's the hair," he says, "out of the head of the Queen of Sleepy Island. So you know where she is," he says, "and I'm going to order you now," he says, "to go and fetch her here first light in the mornin'."

So the king's son went down first light in the morning. Went into the stable. The horse turns 'round and he says, "Do you see the trouble you've gotten me into now? Didn't I tell you," he says, "not to open your mouth when we crossed the crooked-back bridge? Now," he says, "we have to go to Sleepy Island."

"Well," says the king's son, "as long as you know the way," says he, "sure, it'll not take us too long to go."

He says, "I know the way, all right, but," he says, "you were never on Sleepy Island. And I'll tell you what it is. The people on Sleepy Island sleep for twenty years, and then they stay awake for twenty years. Now, if we're very lucky, they'll all be asleep. But we have to get into the island, and," he says, "there's a wall twenty foot high, and it's built with spears. So I'll have to jump over the wall, and if we miss jumping over the wall, we'll come down on the spears, and we'll all be, be killed."

So, the horse went to Sleepy Island. They come to the wall of spears, and the horse made one tremendous jump, and jumped over the wall and landed in the courtyard.

And when they landed in the courtyard, everybody was sleepin'. All the servants was sleepin'. They went into the castle. He opened a door. Sleepin' there. Sleepin' here. Sleepin' every place. And, he went into this room, and he opened it, and there she was layin' on the bed, sleepin', and her hair all shinin' like gold.

And he was just about to pick her up to take her out when she wakened up. And the minute she wakened up, everybody in the castle wakened up. And he was seized and had to give an account of himself. And the servants said, "We'll put him to death."

"No," she says, "put him in the dungeon, and," she says, "tomorrow I'll give my decision."

So he stepped in the dungeon all night and the next day he was taken out. And she says, "I'll pardon you," she says, "if you can riddle me three riddles." Then she considered for a minute. She says, "I'll set you three tasks instead." Uh, she says, "I'm going to hide myself today. And if you can find me," she says, "that'll be one up for you and two down for me. And then," she says, "if you find me, I'll hide meself tomorrow. And if you can find me," she says, "that'll be two up for you, and one down for me. And on the third day," she says, "I'll hide meself again, and if you can find me," she says, "that'll be three up for you, and all down for me," she says, "and I'll go with you wherever you wish."

So, down the man went to the horse, and he says, "I'm in awful bad trouble."

The horse..., "You needn't tell me. You opened your mouth," says he, "when we crossed the crooked-backed bridge."

He says, uh, "The queen's going to hide herself."

Says—says the king's son, "That's right. How do you know that?"

He says, "I know everything. She's going to hide herself, and you don't know where she's going to hide herself. And you have got to find her. Well," he says, "I'm going to tell you where she's going to be hid. She's going to be in the big apple, on the top of the last tree, in the orchard."

"Oh," says the king's son, "that's great! I'll go and...."

"No," says he, "don't do that. If you run out now and goes down there, they'll know that there's something wrong. You look every place until the sun is settin'. When the sun starts to set, go down the orchard, and you'll find her. But don't find her in a hurry."

So he looked everyplace, and upstairs and downstairs, and in the stable, and all 'round the place. Pretendin'. Lookin' for her. But he didn't find her. And then he went down in the orchard, and all these servants was watchin' him. And when he went down, he says, "Oh, lovely apples," and all. And, "I'd love an apple," he says. And the servant put up his hand to pull. "No," he says, "don't pull that one. I want that big apple," he says, "there."

"Oh," the servant says, "you can't get that big apple. Her ladyship wants that apple."

"It doesn't matter," he says. "I want that apple."

And he shook the tree, and the apple fell down. And he had a sword, and he was going to hit the apple to cut it in two. And just as he put up the sword, the servant shouted, "Oh, don't!" And he went over, and she come out—she come out of the apple. Intact.

So, the next day, she hid herself again. And he had to go to the horse the second day. He says, "Where'll she be today?"

Says he, "She's going to be in the brown duck swimmin' on the pond."

So, he looked every place the next day, and, uh, in the evening time he went down to the pond. And there's a whole lot of, uh, lovely black ducks, and white ducks, and one big brown duck swimmin' in the pond. "Oh, Lord!" says the king's son, "I never saw as big a duck. Fetch me a gun!"

But the servant says, "No. That belongs to her ladyship. You daren't."

"Fetch me a gun," he says "I'll shoot—I'll get a gun," he says, "and shoot it."

So he went and he got the gun, and he's just putting the gun up to shoot, when the servant pulled it down, and he says, "Come on. You may come out. He knows where you are." So she come out of the duck.

The third day she went down—he went down to the horse, and he says, "This is the third and last day. Two up now, and one to go." Says he, "Do you know where she's going to be tomorrow?"

"She's going to be under the seventh nail on the front foot of the black mare in the low stable." So, he looked every place and, uh—pretended he was lookin' for her. Comin' on evening, he went down into the stable and he was lookin' and he says, "Oh, Lord, there's an awful fine mare!" He says to the man, "Take that mare out and take her—give her a run 'round. I want to see the—her movements."

So, he took her out, and he trotted her all around, and he come in. He says, "That mare's lame."

"Oh, no," says the servant, "she's not."

"Oh," he says, "she's lame on that left foot." He says, "Fetch me a pliers," he says, "here, ah, till I pull the nail," he says. "And I'll redrive—I'll redrive the nail."

So he pulled out the nail, you see. And he got this big, pointy nail, and he was going to drive it in, and when he went to drive it in, she shouted, "I'm here! Let me out!"

Appendix IV

So, he let her out. So away she went with him, to the King of France. All on the one—this mighty horse. And when they landed with the King of France, he wanted—she wa—he wanted to marry her—the king did. And she would have nothing to do with him until she got three bottles of water from above and beyond the edge of the earth. And the King of France turns to the other king's son, and he says, "Fetch me three bottles of water from above and beyond the edge of the earth."

So the poor fellow went down to the stables, to the black horse, and he says, "Do you know what they want me to do now?"

"I do," he says—the horse. "You have to go 'way to," he says, "to get three bottles of water from above and beyond the edge of the earth."

"Do you know where it is?"

"I do," says the horse. "But if you hadn't opened your mouth," says he, "when we crossed the crooked-backed bridge, we would have no call to get—to do this."

Got on his back. And they galloped away till they come to the edge of the earth. When they come to the edge of the earth there was a fire, with flames going up as high as you could see into the sky. A wall of fire. "This is as far," says the horse, "as I can go. I can't go beyond that fire. And this is the plan. Take out your sword," he says, "and kill me. And leave me carcass lying on the ground. And skin—take the skin off it. And roll the skin back. And," he says, "hide yourself close by. And," he says, "three crows will come," he says, "to peck at my carcass. And when they light on the skin," he, he says, "put out your hand, brave and quick, and catch the three crows. Tell those three crows to fetch you a bottle of water each from above and beyond the edge of the earth."

So he did what he was told. He killed the horse and he skinned him. He rolled himself up in the skin and whenever the three crows come, he put out his hand, and he caught them. He told the three crows, "Fetch me three bottles of water."

The poor old crows flew up, and up, and up, and flew across the flames, and come back with three bottles of water. And when they come back with the three bottles of water, they were all scorched, and their feathers were all singed and everything after flyin' through the fire.

Uh, he dug a great hole for to bury the horse. And he took one of the bottles of water, and he shook a wee taste on the horse, just out of respect. And the minute he shook the water on the horse, the skin went back on him, and the horse jumped up, and he was alive. "You're an awful mean man," says the horse to the king's son. "Why didn't you throw," he says, "a wee taste of that water on them poor crows," he says, "that went to such bother to get that water," he says. And he threw the stuff, and the feathers all grew on them, and away they flew.

Took the three bottles of water back, and when he was putting the horse in the stable, the horse says, "Leave one of them bottles there in the stable with me, and fill another bottle," says he, "out of the well. And take that up," he says, "and give it to the king. And give her ladyship," he says, "that other bottle."

Up he went, and he give the ki—the king the well water. And he kept a bottle himself. And the queen kept the other bottle. And, when she got the water, she says—There was a great big, uh—She had a great big, uh, container of boiling oil—cauldron of boiling oil. Plump and boilin'. And she poured some of the water over her head. And she jumped into it. And she put her head away down underneath it. And she jumped out of it again. And there wasn't even a blister on 'er with this water.

"Now," she says, "anyone else," she says, "that can do that, I'll marry them."

So the king got his bottle of water and put it over his head. But it was only well water, so when he jumped in, he was burned to a cylinder.

And she got very bold. She says, "Anyone else," she says, "that can do that?"

So, he had this bottle, and he poured it over his head. And he jumped in. And he come out the way he went in. And, she married the king, Irish king's son, and they lived very happy ever after.

FRANCIS ("FRANCIE") KENNELLY

The Gentlemen's Agreement

Out there in Spanish Point—I suppose you know it? [CH: Yes, I do.] Couple of hundred yards now, where the president of Ireland was born. [CH: Hillery.] Yes, Doctor Paddy Hillery. There was a man living there, and he had a big family. He had eight or nine in, in family. Boys and girls and every way. But they immigrated, some of 'em. They went to Australia, and they went to America, and they went every place. He was only a small farmer. He had the place of a cow and a mule. That's all he had.

But he was a road contractor as well. Uh, he used to make four miles of a road, like. And the money, the adopted money that was over the four miles of a road, was seventeen pounds thirteen and four pence. But he had this—she had this boy at home, and there was a couple of girls there. He was a great boy. He was a football kicker, and he was a mighty worker. 'Twas he used trim the roads. The roads had to be trimmed. The lough spits had to be trimmed. He had to break two hundred yards of stones and put 'em out in what they called recesses, and spread 'em at the end of the year. But he was well able for it. 'Twas no trouble in the world to him to break three yards of stones in a day.

Well, he, what they call—They had what they call that time a "neddy hammer." There was a twelve ounce and an eight ounce neddy in it. And you see, if you were breakin' heavy stones, you'd have the twelve ounce neddy. And if you're breakin' the lighter stones, do you see, you'd have the, the other....[CH: Different—different ends.] Yes. Yeah. But, uh....[CH: What is it called again?] A neddy hammer. A neddy. Well—I don't know how now is that the right name, but that's the name they were called. But, 'twas no bother to this boy. He used do terrible work. They used rise seaweed as well and make kelp. And they had a great stumble of a black [back?] garden.

But, things were, things were going according to plan. Indeed they were. They were kind of all right. There was a bit of money coming from America, and this was a great boy. The money of the road was coming in, and they had the milk of the cow, and all that.

But this day, in the month of July, he was breakin' stones, and he was never going as good. He was stripped to the shirt now, a grand warm day, and he was, he was thinkin' that he'd beat the three yards that day—that he'd break more, he was goin' so well. This fine girl passed now, as fine as a man ever looked at. And a lot of people used pass Spanish Point. 'Twas a holiday resort even that time. 'Twas all English was here like, and...he was surprised, this girl, she said, "God bless the work!"

"God," he said, "that's strange anyway. On you too," says he.

But she walked down the road in front of him. And he looked after her, and he thought she was the finest girl he ever saw. No more bother now in the world to her, to—Miss Ireland or Miss Universe. Any of them things would be no more bother to her, she was such a fine girl.

She went away, anyway. And he was breakin' away, but I suppose he was thinkin' of the girl away. Naturally enough. And this man came. A fine looking man. A grand suit of clothes. A tailor-made suit and a grand pair of brown shoes. And a Duffy hat. They were in style at the time. Collar and tie and all. Dressed, dressed grand. Well, he didn't say "God bless the work," but he spoke to him.

But, they were talking for a start anyway, and he said to him—But the young fella that was breakin' the stones noticed one thing about him, that he had very, very dangerous eyes. Shifty, kind of dangerous eyes. He was giving him the white of the eye a little bit. But, uh, they spoke for a start anyway, and he, this man said to him, "I saw you looking at that grand girl that passed," said he.

"Oh God," says the young fellow, "why wouldn't anyone?"

"Well, listen," says he, "in two hours time," says he, "make up your mind, and I'll put you—I'll, I'll get you to marry that girl," says he. By God, the young fellow was thinking in himself anyway.

"I'll be back in two hours now," says he. "But one condition," says he, "that you must sell your soul."

By God, sure, he put the young fellow thinkin'. He was thinkin' of the grand girl.

"She's very well off, too," says he. "She has a mighty farm of land and the world of money."

The fella did come back in two hours, and I suppose the young fella was rippin' knots, and the girl came back again. Walkin' this way, like—against him. Whatever way she looked, the time before, she was ten times better looking this time.

By God, anyway, your man landed—the, the devil. He was the devil, do you see? He was dressed, dressed in civilian's clothes. Now all the pictures you saw of the devil, he had a pair of horns and a tail, didn't he? But not this time. He was dressed in civilian's clothes, beautiful clothes. By God, they were....

"Have you my—an answer ready for me?" he said to the young fella.

"Give me a chance," said the young fella. "Give me another hour," he said.

He came back again in another hour, and damn it, wasn't the young fella tempted, and didn't he, didn't he sign on with him.

"Okay," says the devil, says he, "be here," says he, "tomorrow, again," says he. "We'll have no writin' drawn, but we'll, we'll settle it up," says he. "You'll, you'll give me your word," says he. "You're word is your bond," says he, "today ten years I can claim your soul," he said.

"Okay", says the fella.

There was—'twas a gentleman's agreement. They shook hands. They shook hands like that. 'Twas a gentleman's agreement. And 'twas a deal anyway.

But the girl came back the following day. And the talk started anyway, and he couldn't keep her away from the heap of stones. She was so—'tis, I suppose, the, the, the, the, the, the devil had something done, like. They talked away anyway.

By God, the young fella was a bit shy with this grand girl, of course, and she came back the following day. By God, he, as the Americans say, he, he started taking her out in the nights. In the nights anyway. [CH: Dating.] Ah, dating, dating. Things were going, going according to perfection.

Appendix IV

But the house she was staying, the people noticed she was hardly eatin' anything, she was so, so much in love. Then they noticed. They twigged him at home, too. He wasn't eatin' either. The mother twigged him anyway. He had an awful appetite, sure, a man like that. He had an awful appetite. But, the mother twigged him anyhow, but he was giving all kinds of excuses, do you see, but he was meeting the girl, anyway, but she was going to be going home after the holiday. And, by God, he said that this couldn't last anyway. They agreed to marry.

He left Spanish Point, anyway, and she was from County Limerick. They went down to whatever chapel in County Limerick she was from, and they married straight away. Following day—there was no such thing as honeymoons that time—he went out in the farm. But if he did, his eyes opened. She had the place of thirty cows. Thirty calves. Thirty year-and-a-halfs. Thirty two-and-a-halfs. Forty ewes and their lambs and seven sows. There was nine or ten men working for her in this big farm now. They were herdsmen. They were getting very little pay. They had houses. They were called herdsmen. They had houses, and bits of gardens and things from her.

By God, his eyes opened, anyway. He started to go out and work along with them, anyway, and God, with the cattle, and with everything, there was eleven or twelve acres of tillage there. There was three or four farm horses there, and there was this fine hunting horse she was.... She was for—'twas a big change. She used ride up the *scairtín* [a thicket] hounds. She used ride to the hounds. And the—Sure, they were all, I suppose, looking at this fella anyway. But he was a fine boy, and he got on great with 'em.

One year went, and two years went, and three years went, but finally he was married nine years, and he had nine children. Yeah. He was—he had nine children. But, he started...Ah, he was a great worker, and he got very rich, anyway. He got very rich. But, he started to give in the appetite and get thin and shook lookin'. The wife noticed him, and she was bringing him to doctors and things, but no good. He was givin', and givin', and givin'. I suppose he was worryin'—the man was worryin' a bit. Yeah. Nine and a half years went anyway, and he was still the same. He was working away, but he was only just there. Worryin'. Worryin'. Worryin' had had him killed.

But they went to Mass this Sunday, in whatever church they used to go to, and there was stations published for his house. You heard of stations, did you? [CH: Yes.] Yes. There was stations published for his house. And, the woman, his wife now, the woman, the mother of the nine children, she stayed back after Mass, like, to talk to the priest to know, to know what kind of meat they'd like, and things like that, and the breakfast after the stations. [CH: So they had Mass in the house.] They had Mass in the house. The stations, of course. Yeah. They would be twice a year here, every place. The stations.

But, uh, she spoke to him, anyway. "Well, 'tisn't, 'tisn't about that entirely at all," says she, "but I remark my husband," says she. "He's given terrible. And I have him brought to blessed wells," she said, "and doctors, and everything, and no good."

"Ah, my man—my woman," says he—he was a young curate now—"I'm only in the parish six months, and I have that man under observation," says he. "That man is in terrible trouble," says he.

"How?" says she.

"I won't tell you," says he, "now if himself don't tell you."

They went to the stations. He landed with the—this young curate landed with his horse and saddle anyway. All the people used to go to confession in the country house, do you see. He told her, "If I can get that man to make a right confession, we might do something," says he.

The man went in to him anyway, her husband, when the most of the rest of 'em was gone. And, by God, he confessed it. He told her up and down the way this thing happened. "Ah," says the, says the priest, "You"—says the priest to him—"You're in a bad way," says he. "There's only one hope now," says he, "and 'tis very frail," says he. "But, for your penance now," says he—and, sure, the poor man was expecting a terrible penance—"tell your wife," says he, "the very minute, this very minute now this is over today, the stations. Before you go to communion, though," he said. "Tell your wife you should do the penance before you go to communion."

He called out the wife, anyway. Whatever slant he got of her there was—before the Mass was on he told her the whole story. Sure, she nearly dropped dead, she did. She nearly dropped dead anyway. But he went through with the mass anyway, and he received Holy Communion.

And, when the crowd left anyway, they stayed a long time. There used be a big day at the stations. Herself and himself and the priest and the children was gone out around. They went into this room anyway, and they thrashed it out again. "You'll have to go back again," says he, "to that very spot where you made that deal," he said. "And I'll go with you," says he. "And two or three of the priests from—a couple of the priests from Miltown, we'll have to have 'em," says he. "There's only one hope now," says he, "and if that fail, you're done," says he. "You're, you're done," says he. "You're, you're....'Twas a gentleman's deal," says he, "And one word, and one of your words is as good as another."

They tackled up the horse and side-car, anyway, and himself and the wife and the curate. They came from Limerick on, the whole way on to Spanish Point. They landed abroad in Spanish Point, and he showed him the place. Of course, things had changed where he was breakin' the stones. Yerra, he told him before he left Limerick to bring a good spade with him. He brought a spade, anyway. He dug three—or he dug one ring around there now like the table. Of course, a way bigger now. A way bigger than this room, like. A round ring. He shook the holy water around, did the priest, and he read off of the holy books. "Make another," says he. He dug another. He was well able. Around again. That was the second ring. [CH: Around the outside.] Around the outside, yeah.

And, uh, he uh, when he had that done, anyway, the priest put the, shook the holy water again. He read off of the books again, the, the holy books. "No good," says he. "You must dig another." So, the power of the devil must be strong.

He did dig another, anyway, and he shook the holy water, and he read out of the books, anyway. And, uh, "We might do now," says he, "but 'tis only a might," says he. "You stand inside there in that ring now," says he. "Right in the middle of it. And I'll stand near you," says he.

By God, the time was up anyway. They settled the time and all for this now. Something like two o'clock or three o'clock, I don't know which now. But no trace of the devil. 'Twas seven—They were lookin' at the watches. 'Twas them kind of watches they had that time. Seven. Then five minutes. No trace of him. Four minutes. Three minutes. And about two minutes—He was right punctual. They looked out in the sea, and there was a barrel comin', and the sea was rough the same day. And it risin' with the waves, and it all fire. This wave, anyway, rosed. 'Twas comin' in in the shore, and it landed down in the sand, and out walked my man. The very same as he was the day before. Come up to the people, anyway.

"Come on, my man," says he. "We made a deal here ten—this very minute ten years ago. We made a deal. You're—you must come with me," says he. "You sold your soul."

"Hold on," says the priest, "one second now," says he. "You must answer one question for me," says he. And game enough the devil was, he said he would. He was on "Cross Country Quiz" for once in his life, anyway. He might be never in it before, but he said he would. Sure, he thought 'twas a cake walk, do you see.

"Well, now," says the priest—and he standin' up inside in the, in the middle of the ring...[unintelligible]..."There a town in there called Miltown," says he, pointin' in from Spanish Point towards Miltown.

"There is," says the devil. "I know it well," says he. "That's one of my strongholds," says he. "All the people there around, they're boozers, and women loose around the town and everything. Only for that place we'd have to close down altogether," says he. That made the situation, sure, a lot worse.

"You must—But take, for instance, now," says he, "there's a fair there tomorrow."

"Right," says the devil, "there's be fairs there. There's be fairs there often," says he.

"And a man goes in with a good cow," he said. "Listen, now," says he. The devil did. "Listen." He cocked his ear now, and stood to attention, and he listened.

"This man goes into the fair," says he, "with his cow. A good springin' cow," says he. Cattle used be cheap that time. "And he sells this cow at twelve pounds," he said. "Shoves up in the middle of the street now, in a good place, and he sells this cow at twelve pounds, and he's well satisfied. Well, satisfied," he said. Cow was marked and all, and he get's the ticket. They used give tickets that time, the price of the cow, and the man's name that'd buy your cow. And, uh, he'd the ticket marked and all.

And he told him when the, the railway—the railway was goin' at the time—when the railway'd open in the morn—whenever, in an hour's time—"Go up with that cow and get her railed," he said. "There's a man above to take her," he said.

"Okay," says the man.

But this other man came in anyway, and he wanted the cow, and he liked the cow. But he gave him fourteen pounds for the cow. He ducked the, the first fella, do you see? And I suppose they drug the first cow in a yard or something, and the man paid him. Paid him his fourteen pounds, you see. [CH: Right. So the other man lost out?]

Yeah, the other man—And he said to the devil now, "Which of them two men," he said, "would you think was entitled to that cow?" he said.

Ah, the devil answered very quick. "The first man," he said.

"There's where you're wrong," says the priest. "Our Lord died on the cross," he said, "to save that man away back a hundred, one thousand—over a thousand years ago," says he. "You're only the second man."

But with that the devil got frantic. He was—there was fire and brimstone goin' with him. He went on in the barrel, and it was going thirty feet up with every wave out to sea. And he was never seen in Spanish Point since. But if you go out tomorrow—I haven't time to go with you—but if I could go out and show you, there's a burned patch where them three rings is that'll never, never a rib of grass grow in it. There is, uh-huh. [CH: Out near Spanish Point?] Out near Spanish Point. [CH: They're still there?] They're—'Tis still there. It might be, 'tis gone away with the sea now, part of it. Erosion. [CH: When did this happen?] Ah, this happened...'Twould be over a hundred years ago. Uh-huh. 'Twould be over....

Well that isn't the best of it at all, now. There's a bit of a tail-end to that story. I don't come into Miltown but seldom. But I was coming in to the Willie Clancy week there, three or four years ago, and this fellow hopped out across the wall above. He was in a tent. And I was talkin' away to him, and I said, "How'd you like this festival?" He liked it great, he said. He was learnin' the fiddle. There was old classes there. I asked him his name. And, as sure as you're born, he was about the—the fella that, uh, the fella that left Spanish Point was his father, according to the name. Now I didn't question him now, but according to the name and the place he told me he was from in Limerick. [CH: Huh. Did you tell him anything about the...?] I did not. I did not. 'Twas after I was thinking of it. [CH: Yeah. It's better not to say anything anyway.] Yeah, yeah. 'Tis. 'Tis.

Bibliography

Almqvist, Bo. "The Fisherman in Heaven." *Béaloideas* 39-41 (1971-73): 1-55.

──────. "The Irish Folklore Commission: Achievement and Legacy." *Béaloideas* 45-47 (1977-79): 6-26.

Béaloideas: A Journal of the Folklore of Ireland Society. Dublin: Folklore of Ireland Society, 1928-present.

Brown, Terence. *Ireland: A Social and Cultural History, 1922-79*. Glasgow: Fontana, 1981.

Capolungo, Michele. "The Heritage of the Cuchulain Legend in the Modern Irish Ireland of W. B. Yeats and P. H. Pearse." Master's thesis, Centre de Recherches Théatre et Société, Université de Provence—Centre d'Aix.

Carleton, William. *Traits and Stories of the Irish Peasantry*. 1st ser. Dublin, 1830; 2d ser. Dublin, 1838; 5th ed. 2 vols. London: George Routledge & Co., 1856.

Connolly, S. J. *Priests and People in Pre-Famine Ireland, 1780-1845*. Dublin: Gill and Macmillan, 1982.

Corduff, Michael. "Notes on Storytellers and Storytelling in Iorrus, North Mayo." *Béaloideas* 19 (November-December 1949): 177-80.

Court, Artelia. *Puck of the Droms*. Berkeley and Los Angeles: University of California Press, 1985.

Croker, T. Crofton. *Fairy Legends and Traditions of the South of Ireland*. London: John Murray, 1825; rev. ed., London: William Tegg, 1862.

Croker, T. Crofton, and Clifford, Sigerson. *Legends of Kerry*. Tralee, Co. Kerry: The Geraldine Press, 1972.

Cross, Tom Peete. *Motif-Index of Early Irish Literature*. Indiana University Folklore Series, no. 7. Bloomington, Indiana: Indiana University Press, 1952.

Curtin, Jeremiah. *Hero-Tales of Ireland*. London: Macmillan & Co., 1894.

_____. *Myths and Folk-Lore of Ireland*. London: Macmillan & Co., 1890; reprint ed., New York: Weathervane Books, 1975.

_____. *Tales of the Fairies and of the Ghost World Collected from Oral Tradition in South-West Munster*. London: Alfred Nutt, 1895.

de Bhaldraithe, Tomás, ed. *Seanchas Thomáis Leighléis*. Baile Átha Cliath: An Clóchomar Tta., 1977.

Delargy, J. H. "The Gaelic Story-Teller. With Some Notes on Gaelic Folk-Tales." *Proceedings of the British Academy* 31 (1945): 177-221.

Dorson, Richard M. Foreword to *Folktales of Ireland*, ed. Sean O'Sullivan. Chicago: University of Chicago Press, 1966.

Edgeworth, Maria. *Castle Rackrent*. London: Joseph Johnson, 1800.

Edwards, Ruth Dudley. *An Atlas of Irish History*. London: Methuen & Co., 1973; reprint ed., London and New York: Methuen & Co., 1981.

Evans, E. Estyn. *Irish Folk Ways*. London: Routledge and Kegan Paul, 1957.

Folktales of Ireland, ed. Sean O'Sullivan. Chicago: University of Chicago Press, 1966.

Ford, Patrick K. "Competence and Competition in Irish Storytelling Tradition." Paper presented at the annual meeting of the Modern Language Association, Houston, Texas, December 1980.

_____. "You Just Come to Me and I'll Blind You with Irish." *Folklore and Mythology* (July 1984): 1.

Funk and Wagnalls Standard Dictionary of Folklore, Mythology, and Legend, ed. Maria Leach. 1972 ed., vol. 1, s.v. "Folklore."

Glassie, Henry. *Irish Folk History*. Philadelphia: University of Pennsylvania Press, 1982.

_____. *Irish Folktales*. New York: Pantheon Books, 1985.

_____. *Passing the Time in Ballymenone: Culture and History of an Ulster Community*. Philadelphia: University of Pennsylvania Press, 1982.

Gregory, Lady Augusta. *Visions and Beliefs in the West of Ireland*. 2 vols. New York: 1920; reprint ed., Gerrard's Cross, Buckinghamshire: Colin Smythe, 1970.

Gribben, Arthur. "The Role of the Ancient Irish Epic *Táin Bó Cuailnge* in the Sense of Local Cultural Identity in Contemporary North County Louth, Ireland." Ph.D. diss., University of California, Los Angeles, 1988.

Handler, Richard, and Linnekin, Jocelyn. "Tradition, Genuine or Spurious." *Journal of American Folklore* 97 (July-September 1984): 273-90.

Harvey, Clodagh Brennan. "Some Irish Women Storytellers and Reflections on the Role of Women in the Storytelling Tradition." *Western Folklore* 48 (1989): 109-28.

Harvey, Clodagh M. "A Contemporary Perspective on Irish Traditional Storytelling in the English Language." Ph.D. dissertation, University of California, Los Angeles, 1987.

Hernadi, Paul. "The Erotics of Retrospection: Historytelling, Audience Response, and the Strategies of Desire." *New Literary History* 12 (Winter 1981): 243-52.

Hyde, Douglas. *Beside the Fire: A Collection of Irish Gaelic Folk Stories*. London: David Nutt, 1890.

_____. *Legends of Saints and Sinners*. Dublin: The Talbot Press, 1915.

Hymes, Dell. "Breakthrough into Performance." In *Folklore: Performance and Communication*, edited by Dan Ben-Amos and Kenneth Goldstein, 11-74. The Hague: Mouton & Co., 1975.

Ireland's Own: A Journal of Fiction, Literature, and General Information. Dublin: 1902-present.

Johnson, Paul. *Ireland: A Concise History from the Twelfth Century to the Present Day*. London: Granada, 1981.

Kinsella, Thomas, trans. *The Tain*. Dublin: Dolmen Press, 1969.

Larminie, William. *West Irish Folk-Tales and Romances*. London, n.p., 1893; reprint ed., Freeport, New York: Books for Libraries Press, 1972.

Linton, Ralph. "Nativistic Movements." *American Anthropologist* 45 (1943): 230-40.

MacCall, Seamus. *A Little History of Ireland*. Portlaoise, Co. Laois: The Dolmen Press, 1973.

MacKillop, James. "Finn Mac Cool: The Hero and Anti-Hero in Irish Folk Tradition." In *Views of the Irish Peasantry*, edited by Daniel J. Casey and Robert E. Rhodes, 86-106. Hamden, Conn.: Archon Books, 1977.

Mercier, Vivian. *The Irish Comic Tradition*. Oxford: Oxford University Press, 1962.

Millman, Lawrence. *Our Like Will Not Be There Again*. Boston: Little, Brown & Co., 1977.

Neill, Kenneth. *The Irish People: An Illustrated History*. New York: Mayflower Books, 1979.

Ní Dhuibhne, Éilís. "Dublin Modern Legends: An Intermediate Type List and Examples." *Béaloideas* 51 (1983): 55-70.

Nicolaisen, W. F. H. "Concepts of Time and Space in Irish Folktales." In *Celtic Folklore and Christianity: Studies in Memory of William H. Heist*, edited by Patrick K. Ford, 150-58. Santa Barbara, Calif.: McNally & Loftin, 1983.

Ó Catháin, Séamas. *The Bedside Book of Irish Folklore*. Dublin and Cork: The Mercier Press, 1980.

_____. *Irish Life and Lore*. Dublin and Cork: The Mercier Press, 1982.

Ó Cathasaigh, Seán. "Buailíochaí in iathar Chonamara." *Béaloideas* 13 (1943): 159-60.

Ó Coileáin, Seán. "Oral vs. Literary? Some Strands of the Argument." *Studia Hibernica* 17-18 (1977-78): 7-35.

Ó Danachair, Caoimhín. "The Irish Folklore Commission." *The Folklore and Folk Music Archivist* 1 (Spring 1961): 1.

_____. "Oral Tradition and the Printed Word." *Irish University Review* 9 (Spring 1979): 31-41.

Ó Domhnaill, Seán. *Seal ag Léamh* [Reading Time]. Baile Átha Cliath: An Comhlacht Oideachais, 1977.

Ó Duilearga, Séamus. "Paddy Sherlock's Stories." *Béaloideas* 30 (1962): 1-75.

_____, ed. *Leabhar Sheáin Í Chonaill*. Baile Átha Cliath: Comhairle Bhéaloideas Éireann, 1948.

_____, ed. *Leabhar Stiofáin Uí Ealaoire*. Baile Átha Cliath: Comhairle Bhéaloideas Éireann, 1981.

_____, ed. *Seán Ó Conaill's Book*. Translated by Máire MacNeill. Baile Átha Cliath: Comhairle Bhéaloideas Éireann, 1981.

Ó hEochaidh, Seán. "Buailteachas i dTír Chonaill." *Béaloideas* 13 (1943): 130-58.

_____. *Síscéalta Ó Thír Chonaill*. Translated by Máire MacNeill; edited by Séamas Ó Catháin. Dublin: Comhairle Bhéaloideas Éireann, 1977.

Ó Moghráin, Pádraig. "Some Mayo Traditions of the *Buaile*." *Béaloideas* 13 (1943): 161-71.

Ó Súilleabháin, Seán. *A Handbook of Irish Folklore*. Dublin: Folklore of Ireland Society, 1942; reprint ed., Hatboro, Penn.: Folklore Associates, 1963.

_____. Introduction to *Folktales of Ireland*, ed. Sean O'Sullivan. Chicago: University of Chicago Press, 1966.

_____. *Irish Wake Amusements*. Dublin and Cork: The Mercier Press, 1967.

Ó Súilleabháin, Seán, and Christiansen, Reidar Th. *The Types of the Irish Folktale*. Folklore Fellows Communications, no. 188. Helsinki, 1963.

O'Sullivan, Sean. *Legends from Ireland*. London: B. T. Batsford, 1977.

_____, ed. *Folktales of Ireland*. Chicago: University of Chicago Press, 1966.

The Oxford English Dictionary, 1961 ed., s.v. "Sennachie."

Schafer, Roy. "Action and Narration in Psychoanalysis." *New Literary History* 12 (Autumn 1980): 61-85.

The Shanachie: An Irish Miscellany [subtitle varies]. 2 vols. Dublin: Maunsel & Co., 1906-7.

Shiel, Michael J. *The Quiet Revolution*. Dublin: The O'Brien Press, 1984.

Thompson, Stith. *Motif-Index of Folk-Literature*. Rev. ed. 6 vols. Bloomington, Indiana: Indiana University Press, 1955-58.

_____. *The Types of the Folktale: A Classification and Bibliography*. 2d rev. Folklore Fellows Communications, no. 184. Helsinki, 1961.

Toelken, J. Barre. "The 'Pretty Language' of Yellowman: Genre, Mode, and Texture in Navaho Coyote Narratives." *Genre* 2 (1969): 211-35.

_____. "Seeing with a Native Eye: How Many Sheep Will It Hold?" In *Seeing with a Native Eye: Essays on Native American Religion*, edited by Walter Holden Capps, 9-24. New York: Harper & Row, 1976.

Von Sydow, C. W. "Geography and Folk-Tale Oicotypes." In *Selected Papers on Folklore*, edited by Laurits Bødker, 44-59. Copenhagen: Rosenkilde & Bagger, 1948; reprint ed., New York: Arno Press, 1977.

Waters, Martin J. "Peasants and Emigrants: Considerations of the Gaelic League as a Social Movement." In *Views of the Irish Peasantry*, edited by Daniel J. Casey and Robert E. Rhodes, 160-77. Hamden, Conn.: Archon Books, 1977.

Whorf, Benjamin Lee. "Science and Linguistics." In *Language, Thought, and Reality: Selected Writings of Benjamin Lee Whorf*, edited by John B. Carroll, 207-19. Cambridge, Mass.: The Technology Press of Massachusetts Institute of Technology, 1956.

Wilgus, D. K. "Irish Traditional Narrative Songs in English: 1800-1916." In *Views of the Irish Peasantry*, edited by Daniel J. Casey and Robert E. Rhodes, 107-28. Hamden, Conn.: Archon Books, 1977.

Williams, J. E. Caerwyn. *Y Storïwr Gwyddeleg a'i Chwedlau*. Cardiff: University of Wales Press, 1972.

Index

"Above and Beyond the End of the Earth," 64–66, 81n.30
Aesthetic criteria for traditional storytelling, 15–16, 44–45, 54–74, 76–77
Áirneán
    áirneán bean, 12
    áirneán fear, 12
American Folklorists, 14, 77
    Richard Dorson, 25
An Cumann le Béaloideas Éireann, 2
Anderson, Frank, 39–40, 42, 45
Anglo-Irish War, 1
Anglo-Irish writers, 6
Ar cuairt, 7, 21, 23–25, 31, 48
Armagh (south), dialect of, 64
Automobile, impact of, 24, 27

Ballinagare (Co. Roscommon), 39
Ballinskelligs (Co. Kerry), 24, 38
Ballyvaughan (Co. Clare), 10
Belfast Storytelling Festival, 78
Bell Harbour (Co. Clare), 11
Beside the Fire, 53–55
Bicycle, impact of, 23–24, 33n.10
Bilingualism, implications of, 15
Bourke, Elizabeth, 39–40, 45, 75
Bullaun (Co. Galway), 24–25

Cahirsiveen (Co. Kerry), 74
Campbell, John, 8, 11, 16, 28, 31, 38–39, 45–47, 63
    on motivations for storytelling, 56
    storytelling style of, 63–66
Carna (Co. Galway), 11, 24, 28, 74–75, 78, 82n.43
Carún, Seán, 37–38
Ceili bands, 26, 34n.19
Ceili house, 8
Ceiliing, 8
Christianity, 31
Cillrialaigh (Iveragh Peninsula), 7
Civil War, Irish, 1, 29
Cloonfad (Co. Roscommon), 8, 25
Coimisiún Béaloideasa Éireann, 2
Collectors, folklore. *See* Folklore collectors
Comhaltas Ceoltóirí Éireann, 41, 63
Commercial publications, relationship to storytelling tradition, 13
Conceptual framework for study of folklore, 77
Connemara (Co. Galway), 11
Coolea (Co. Cork), 74
Costello, Liam, 23
County Clare, music and storytelling in, 42–45

County Donegal, 48
County Kerry, 7
Crehan, Martin ("Junior"), 16, 40–42, 44, 50n.14, 66, 69–71
Croker, T. Crofton, 54
Crua-Ghaedhilg (or *crua-Ghaolainn*), 55–56
CúChulainn, 13, 19n.46, 76
Cultural identity, 1, 13
Cultural loss, 2
Curtin, Jeremiah, 54

Dance bands, 26
Dance halls, 24–26, 34n.18
Dancing, traditional, 24
Decorum, rules of, 7, 14
Delaney, James, 3, 31
　commentary on "travelers," 9
Delargy, James (Séamas Ó Duilearga), 9, 37–38
　on English language narratives, 36n.37, 55
　on the storytelling tradition, 12
Department of Education (Irish), policy of, 13
Department of Irish Folklore, 3–6, 39, 76
Depopulation, rural, 24, 46
Diction
　in English language narratives, 55–74, 81n.32
　of tales in Irish, 55–59
Documentation, 2, 12–13, 37–42, 47–49
Domestic appliances, ownership of, 22–23, 33n.9
Donohoe, Tom, 32
Doolin (Co. Clare), 37, 43
Dorson, Richard, 25
Droney, Catherine ("Katie"), 11, 40–41, 75
　storytelling style of, 66
Dunmore (Co. Galway), 8
Dunquin (Co. Kerry), 26–27, 43n.21
"Dutch door," 28

Eachtraithe, 7
Easter Rising, the, repercussions of, 1, 29–30
Economic change, 20–23
Ediphone machine, 2, 48
Education, availability of, 24, 28–30
Educational policy, nationalism in, 13–14
Emigration, 24
　commission on, 29
Ennistymon (Co. Clare), 43
Entertainment, in the countryside, 22–27, 29
European Economic Community (EEC), 21
Evans, E. Estyn, 2

"The Fairy Football Match," 69–71, 82n.40
Fanore (Co. Clare), 31
Farmers, small, plight of, 21
"Felix," 71–73, 82n.42
Fenian tales, 3, 47
　Finn Cycle, 12, 13
　women as narrators of, 12, 47, 49
Finnscéalta, 3, 12, 47
Fionn MacCumhail, 13, 76
Folk culture, guide to documentation of, 3, 17n.11
Folklore
　association with rural life, 7, 18n.18
　creation of, 14
Folklore collecting, 24, 37–42, 47–49, 57, 76
　emphases in, 2, 54, 57
　nationalism in, 1–2
Folklore collectors
　activities of, 1–3, 5, 15, 37–42, 48–49, 74–75
　Costello, Liam, 23
　Delaney, James, 3, 9, 31
　as interview subjects, 4
　lack of women, 48–49
　Munnelly, Thomas, 3, 38–42
　Murphy, Michael J., 40
　Murphy, Tadhg, 25
　Ó Catháin, Séamas, 14, 40, 34n.11
　Ó Floinn, Bairbre, 39–40, 42
　Ó hEochaidh, Seán, 32, 48–49, 58
Folklore of Ireland Society, 2
Folklore scholars, Irish, 7, 15, 57–58, 74–78
Folklore scholarship (Irish)
　historical developments in, 1, 17n.1
　issues in, 14, 53
　relationship to storytelling tradition, 74–78
Folktales, Irish, collections of, 4, 25, 53–54
Forkhill (Co. Armagh), 11
Funerals, customs associated with, 26–27

Index

Gaelic culture, legacy of, 2, 13–14, 54
Gaelic League, 1, 34n.18, 53
Gaeltacht (Gaeltachtaí), 2, 24, 55, 57, 74
"The Gentlemen's Agreement," 66–68, 82n.35
Glassie, Henry, 22
Glenflesk (Co. Kerry), 45–46
Gleninagh (Co. Clare), 10, 15, 24, 32, 76
    fishing economy of, 11
Gregory, Lady Augusta, 48

A Handbook of Irish Folklore, 3
"Hard Irish," 55–56
Henry VIII, papers of, 18n.17
Hero tales, 3, 47, 55, 76
    Ulster Cycle, 13
    women as narrators of, 12
Histories, life of storytellers, 4
Homes (Irish), modernization of, 28
Hyde, Douglas, 1, 53–56
Hymes, Dell, 59

Í Shé, Seán Chormaic, 56
Immigrants, returned, 29
Independence, Irish, 1
Institiúd Béaloideasa Éireann, 2
Interview
    results, 20–32, 38–45
    subjects, 4
Inveran (Co. Galway), 23
Ireland's Own, 13, 35n.33
Irish Folklore Commission, 5, 6, 24
    purpose of, 2
Irish Folklore Institute, 2
Irish Folklore Studies, 1, 9, 31, 37–38, 47–49
Irish language, preeminence of storytelling tradition in, 54–58, 76–77

Jazz bands, 26

Kelleher, Peter, 23–25, 40–41, 46–47, 56, 75
Kelly, Eamon
    influence of, 6, 45–47, 51n.20, 64
    as "The Shanachie," 6, 45–46, 51n.19, 75, 78

Kennedy, Patrick, 54
Kennelly, Francis ("Francie"), 16, 27, 39, 42
    storytelling style of, 66–68, 81n.33
Killala (Co. Mayo), 40
Kitchens (Irish), modernization of, 28
"Kruger's" (pub), 26–27, 34n.21

Laighléis, Tomás, 29–30, 34n.22
Language (Irish)
    decline of, 2, 8, 15, 31, 35n.36, 58, 80n.22
    emphasis on materials in, 2, 17n.5
    in Northern Ireland, 84n.60
    preeminence of storytelling tradition in, 53–58
Lenihan, Máirtín, 15, 76
Literacy, in English, 29–30
Literary Revival, Irish, 30, 53
Literary treatment of folktales, 18n.1, 53–54
Loughrea (Co. Galway), 24

"The Mac a hAon Fionn," 62–63, 80–81n.26
MacNeill, Eoin, 1
McCarthy, Patrick ("Pappy"), 10, 24, 29
McDermot, Seán, 23–24
McGann, John ("Jacko"), 42, 69
McKenna, Martin, 8, 31, 38, 66, 75–76
Mahony, Jack, 8, 25, 32, 57, 66
Märchen, 3, 12, 47, 55
Memorial tradition, 14
Menlo (Co. Galway), 23, 29–30
Mercier, Vivian, 33n.10
Miltown Malbay (Co. Clare), 27, 42–43
Mobility, impact of increased, 23–24
Modernization of the countryside, 20–32
Moore, Donal, 12, 16, 24, 38, 44, 56, 74, 76
    storytelling style of, 62, 81n.32
Mortuaries, appearance of, 28–28
Muckross Estate (Co. Kerry), 11
Mullaghbawn (Co. Armagh), 8, 27
Munnelly, Thomas, 3, 38–42
Murphy, Michael J., 40
Murphy, Tadhg, 25
Murrihy, Patrick ("Packie"), 16, 38–39
    storytelling style of, 59–62, 81n.32
Murrough (Co. Clare), 8, 11

Music, traditional
   centers of, 43
   resurgence of, 26, 43–44
   and storytelling tradition, 39, 41–45

Na Cruacha (Co. Donegal), 24, 34n.11, 49
NAPPS, 77
"Narrative time," 66
Narrators
   Anderson, Frank, 39–40, 42, 45
   Bourke, Elizabeth, 39–40, 45, 75
   Campbell, John, 8, 11, 16, 28, 31, 38–39, 45–47, 63, 56, 63–66
   Carún, Seán, 37–38
   Crehan, Martin ("Junior"), 16, 40–42, 44, 50n.14, 66, 69–71
   Droney, Catherine ("Katie"), 11, 40–41, 75, 66
   Í Shé, Seán Chormaic, 56
   Kelleher, Peter, 23–25, 40,–41, 46–47, 56, 75
   Kennelly, Francis ("Francie"), 16, 27, 39, 42
      storytelling style of, 66–68, 81n.33
   Lenihan, Máirtín, 15, 76
   McDermot, Seán, 23–24
   McGann, John ("Jacko"), 42, 69
   McKenna, Martin, 8, 31, 38, 66, 75–76
   Mahony, Jack, 8, 25, 32, 57, 66
   Moore, Donal, 12, 16, 24, 38, 44, 56, 74, 76
   Murrihy, Patrick ("Packie"), 16, 38–39
      storytelling style of, 59–62, 81n.32
   Nestor, Martin, 32, 76
   Nic Aodha, Máire, 24, 32, 49
   O'Brien, Michael ("Mick"), 69
   Ó Conaill, Seán, 7
   Ó Donnghaile, Bartley, 11
   Ó Donnghaile, Éamonn, 11, 28, 31, 58
      on significance of *scéalaí* and *seanchaí*, 74–75
   Ó Duinnín, Seán, 11, 13, 14, 46, 56, 74, 76
   O'Farrell, Patrick, 27, 39–40, 66
   Ó hAirt, Séamas, 56
   Ó hEalaoire, Stiofán, 38, 42, 50n.4
   O'Sullivan, Cáit (narrator), 14, 26, 74–75

Reilly, John, 8, 16, 31–32, 40, 41, 50n.12, 57
   storytelling style of, 71–73
Ryan, Tomáisín, 11
Sherlock, Paddy, 10
Stack, Liam, 26
See also Storytellers
Nationalism, Irish, 1, 53
   development of, 30
   in the popular press, 13, 30
Nestor, Martin, 32, 76
Newspapers, importance of, 10, 28–30
Nic Aodha, Máire, 24, 32, 49
Northern Ireland, 8, 38, 84n.60

O'Brien, Michael ("Mick"), 69
Ó Catháin, Séamas, 14, 40, 34n.11
Ó Conaill, Seán, 7
O'Connell, Michael, 74, 83n.49
Ó Danachair, Caoimhín, 2
Ó Donnghaile, Bartley, 11
Ó Donnghaile, Éamonn, 11, 28, 31, 58
   on significance of *scéalaí* and *seanchaí*, 74–75
O'Donoughoe, Brendan, 10–11
Ó Duilearga, Séamus, 9, 12, 36n.37, 37–38, 55, 56
Ó Duinnín, Seán, 11, 13, 14, 46, 56, 74, 76
O'Farrell, Patrick, 27, 39–40, 66
Ó Floinn, Bairbre, 39–40, 42
Ó hAirt, Séamas, 56
Ó hEalaoire, Stiofán, 38, 42, 50n.4
Ó hEochaidh, Seán, 32, 48–49, 58
Oireachtas, 57–58
Orality, criterion of in folklore studies, 13–14
Ó Rócháin, Muiris, 39
Ó Súilleabháin, Seán, 3
O'Sullivan, Cáit, 14, 26, 74–75

Pale, The, 54, 79n.7
Peasant class
   defined, 33n.2
   predominance of, 21
Performing, vs. reporting, 59
Phonograph (gramophone), 22
   impact of, 25, 34n.13

Index

Poverty in the countryside, 21–22
Printed sources of folktales, 13–14, 19n.46, 30, 76
Public houses ("pubs"), 25–27, 34n.22

"The Quarryman's Son," 60–62, 80n.25
Questionnaire, research, 4–5, 20
Quilty (Co. Clare), 43

Radio, introduction of, 7, 18n.22, 22–25
Radio Telefís Éireann, 7, 23, 84n.61
Ratio, of women to men narrators, 13
Reilly, John, 8, 16, 31–32, 40, 41, 50n.12, 57
    storytelling style of, 71–73
Reporting, 59
"Runs," 55, 58, 80n.15
Rural Electrification Scheme, 25, 34n.18
Rural households, inaccessibility of, 25–26
Rural life, 43
    association of Eamon Kelly with, 6, 45–47
    association with storytelling tradition, 13
    dissatisfaction with, 29
    personal quality of, 27–28
    social isolation of, 25–26
    vs. urban life, 45, 77–78
Ryan, Tomáisín, 11

Scéalaí, 3–5, 47
    social significance of term, 74–75
Scéalaíocht, 3-5, 17n.13, 55, 58, 68–69
    narrating and narrators of, 58–68, 83n.45
Scéalta gaisce, 3, 47, 55
Seanchaí, 4, 18n.17, 47, 51n.19
    social significance of term, 74–75
Seanchas, 4, 5, 17n.13, 58
    medieval, 82–83n.44
    narrators of, 12, 41, 68–74

Sean-sgéalta, 3, 12, 32, 47
Segregation of the sexes, 26, 34n.18, 34n.22
Self-consciousness of the storytelling tradition, 42–45
Sherlock, Paddy, 10
Shiel, Michael J., 21
Showbands, Irish, 26, 34n.19

Síscéalta, 58
Skibbereen (Co. Cork), 3
Social change and the storytelling tradition, 20–32
Stack, Liam, 26
Standard of living
    gap between rural and urban, 23, 45
    rise in, 21–22
Statues of Kilkenny, 79n.7
Stokes, Patrick, self-description, 9
Storyteller, traditional
    self-concept of, 39–41
    defined, 5–6
Storytellers
    American, 77
    criteria for, 5–6
    as interview subjects, 4–5
    social isolation of, 5, 45
    See also Narrators
Storytelling, traditional
    association with rural life, 7, 13, 45
    contexts for, 3–5, 7–13, 22–28, 31–32, 38–42, 44–46, 48–49, 57–58, 63, 77, 80n.21
    presumed conservatism of, 14
Storytelling Festival, International, 38, 39, 77
Storytelling revival, 15, 77
Storytelling tradition
    background to, 7–16
    decline of, 2–3, 13, 22–32, 42, 53–54
    documentation of, 2, 12–13, 37–42, 47–49
    in English, 54–78
    role of women in, 7, 12–13, 47–49
    travelers and the, 9, 11
Styles, storytelling, 58–60, 62–64, 66, 69, 71, 81n.32
Survivals, study of, 76

Táin Bó Cuailnge, 19n.46, 83n.45
Tales, traditional
    of children, 13, 76
    divisions of, 4, 17n.13, 55
    literary uses of, 17n.1, 53–54
    sources of, 4, 12, 13, 15, 30, 76
Technological innovations, 22–25, 27–28

Television, introduction of, 7, 18n.21, 18n.22, 22–24
"Tinkers," 9
Tradition
    Anglo-Irish, 45
    continuity in, 14–15
    preservation of, 1–3, 5, 37–42, 47–49, 53–58, 74–78
Tradition bearers, 4, 37–38
Transcriptions, 2, 16
Transhumance, 48–49
Transmission, process of, 4
"Travelers" (itinerants), 9–11
    Paddy Sherlock, 10
    Patrick Stokes, 9

Ulster, 23, 33n.8
Ulster Cycle, 13
University College Dublin, 3
Urban belief tales, 76

Visiting, custom of, 7–12, 48–49
    changes in, 22–32, 78
Von Sydow, Carl W., 37

Wake customs, 11
    decline of, 27–28, 35n.27
    disapproval of, 11
Waters, Martin, 30
Wilde, Lady Jane, 54
Williams, J. E. Caerwyn, 12–13, 55–56
Willie Clancy Summer School, 39, 44
Women
    limited participation of, 7, 12, 19n.40
    problems in documentation of, 12–13, 47–49
    in public houses, 27, 34n.22
World War I, 24

www.ingramcontent.com/pod-product-compliance
Lightning Source LLC
Chambersburg PA
CBHW082044230426

43670CB00016B/2772